FM 3-37

Field Manual
No. 3-37

Headquarters
Department of the Army
Washington, DC, 30 September 2009

Protection

I0026817

Contents

Distribution Restriction: Approved for public release; distribution is unlimited.

Figures

Tables

Preface

Field Manual (FM) 3-37 provides doctrinal guidance for commanders and staffs who are responsible for planning and executing protection in support of full spectrum operations. It describes protection as both an element of combat power and as a warfighting function. FM 3-37 corresponds with Army operations doctrine introduced in the FM 3-0 capstone manual.

As the Army keystone manual for protection, FM 3-37 will help commanders understand and visualize protection concepts and ideas and enable them to describe protection tasks and systems for integration into the operations process. FM 3-37 expands on the protection and combined arms terminology outlined in FM 3-0. It explains how protection can be achieved and applied through the combination and integration of reinforcement and complementary capabilities to preserve combat power or to protect personnel, physical assets, or information. This manual recognizes that protection has no direct antecedent from the former battlefield operating systems, so protection is realized in many ways. Therefore, the text introduces the five forms and five principles of protection to provide a context for battle command and a framework for task assignment:

- Forms of protection.
  - Deterrence.
  - Prevention.
  - Active security.
  - Passive defense.
  - Mitigation.
- Principles of protection.
  - Full-dimension.
  - Integrated.
  - Layered.
  - Redundant.
  - Enduring.

FM 3-37 also introduces and explains the twelve Army tasks that comprise the protection warfighting function and describes how those tasks are realized and represented during full spectrum operations:

- Air and missile defense (AMD).
- Personnel recovery (PR).
- Information protection.
- Fratricide avoidance.
- Operational area security.
- Antiterrorism (AT).
- Survivability.
- Force health protection (FHP).
- Chemical, biological, radiological, and nuclear (CBRN) operations.
- Safety.
- Operations security (OPSEC).
- Explosive ordnance disposal (EOD).

This manual affirms the composite risk management (CRM) process as the overarching process for integrating protection into Army operations and depicts a broad methodology for determining protection priorities from which specific decision support tools can nest. FM 3-37 provides guidance on how the protection cell within the division, corps, and Army headquarters is formed for protection planning, preparation, execution, and continuous assessment.

Note. It is Department of the Army (DA) policy to develop and employ all measures that prevent attacks and minimize risks from hazards to Soldiers, civilians, their Families, infrastructures, and information to achieve mission assurance. To adapt to an evolving environment and to achieve a broad, coherent, and comprehensive approach to protection, the Army applies an all-hazards approach to protection. This approach focuses on protecting personnel, physical assets, and information from traditional, irregular, disruptive, and catastrophic threats, including criminal activity and naturally occurring disasters. The Army will prepare to recover quickly if prevention and protection efforts fail.

Commanders should be aware that homeland defense and civil support operations in the continental United States (CONUS) are governed by a distinct set of laws and policies regarding the employment of forces, types of operations, and use of force. These laws and policies must be factored into determining the appropriate use of protection principles and tasks and systems for an operation in CONUS.

This manual follows joint doctrine and introduces several ideas to provide a context for understanding protection within the military art and science of operations to achieve its purpose of preserving the force—personnel (combatant and noncombatant), physical assets, and information. FM 3-37 strives for a broad application of some universal concepts regarding protection and also integrates lessons learned from five years of combat operations.

This manual is organized as follows:

- Chapter 1, Preserving the Force.
- Chapter 2, Protection Warfighting Function.
- Chapter 3, Protection in Full Spectrum Operations.
- Chapter 4, Protection Integration in Army Operations.
- Chapter 5, Protection Cells.
- Appendix A, Protection in Force Projection Operations.
- Appendix B, Combat Identification.
- Appendix C, Protection of Military Bases.
- Appendix D, Operations Security.

Definitions for which FM 3-37 is the proponent publication (the authority) are in boldfaced text and have an asterisk in the glossary. These terms and their definitions will be incorporated into the next revision of FM 1-02. For other definitions in the text, the term is italicized and the number of the proponent publication follows the definition.

This publication applies to the Active Army, the Army National Guard (ARNG)/the Army National Guard of the United States (ARNGUS), and the United States Army Reserve (USAR) unless otherwise stated.

The proponent for this publication is the U.S. Army Training and Doctrine Command (TRADOC). Send comments and recommendations on DA Form 2028 (Recommended Changes to Publications and Blank Forms) directly to Commanding General, U.S. Army Maneuver Support Center, ATTN: ATZT-TDD, 320 MANSCEN Loop, Suite 270, Fort Leonard Wood, Missouri 64573-8929. Submit an electronic DA Form 2028 or comments and recommendations in the DA Form 2028 format by e-mail to <leon.mdottdddoc@conus.army mil>.

Unless this publication states otherwise, masculine nouns and pronouns do not refer exclusively to men.

This page intentionally left blank.

Chapter 1

Preserving the Force

Protection of the fighting force is inherent to command. Every military activity, from training and predeployment preparation through mission accomplishment, requires the commander to assume responsibility for protecting the force while achieving the objective. This chapter defines and examines protection as an element of combat power and as a warfighting function. It introduces and discusses the forms and principles of protection and the CRM process. The purpose of these protection constructs, methodologies, and processes is to help frame and organize protection activities for their integration into the operations process where they can facilitate decisionmaking.

PROTECTION ROLE

1-1.   Military activities and operations are intrinsically hazardous. Commanders and leaders conducting full spectrum operations must assume prudent risks every day based on the significance of the mission, the exigency of the operation, and opportunity. In warfare, this reality defines a sacred trust that must exist between leaders and Soldiers regarding mission accomplishment and protection. A commander's inherent duty to protect the force should not lead to risk aversion or inhibit the freedom of action necessary for maintaining initiative and momentum or achieving decisive results during operations. Leaders balance these competing responsibilities and make risk decisions based on experience, ethical and analytical reasoning, and their knowledge of the unit and the situation and through intuitive judgment. It is through protection that commanders and leaders preserve combat power and reduce the risk of loss, damage, or injury to their formations.

> *Note.* In an environment where terrorism persists, protection considerations must be considered in garrison and in preparatory phases to operations.

1-2.   *Protection* **is the preservation of the effectiveness of mission-related military and nonmilitary personnel, equipment, facilities, information, and infrastructure deployed or located within or outside the boundaries of a given operational area.**

1-3.   Protection is an element of combat power and a warfighting function. As a contributor to overall combat power, protection represents relative potential; as a warfighting function, protection refers to twelve specific tasks and systems that are explained in chapter 2. It is easy to confuse these two constructs while conceptualizing, visualizing, or describing protection means and capabilities. Commanders reference protection as an element of combat power when they understand and visualize all possible activities, actions, and effects available for protection. Some of these actions or effects may be achieved through the combined integration of the other five elements of combat power (movement and maneuver, intelligence, fires, sustainment, and command and control [C2]), focused by leadership and information and resulting in an increasingly effective and efficient concept of protection. (See figure 1-1, page 1-2.)

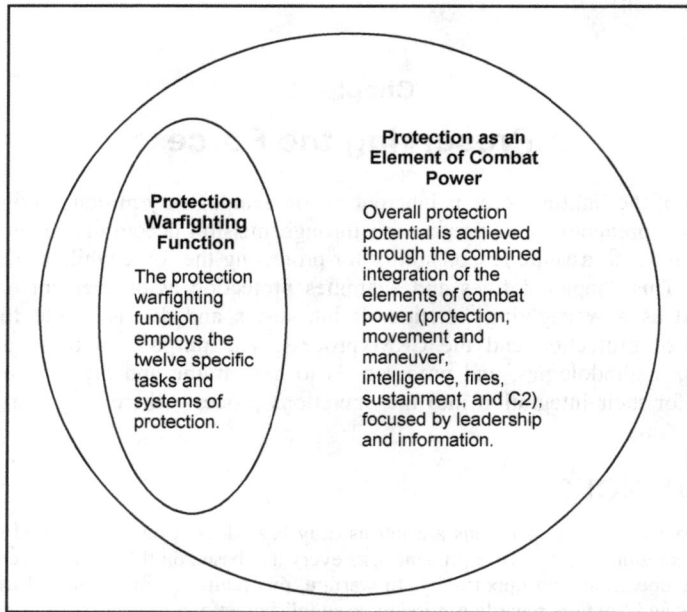

Figure 1-1. Protection as an element of combat power

1-4. Commanders and leaders typically describe or give guidance using the warfighting functions to identify specific tasks from which operations and missions can be developed. The protection warfighting function—

- Serves to specifically focus the broad range of protection activities into quantifiable tasks and relevant systems for simplification, integration, and synchronization in the Army operations process.
- Describes the twelve specific tasks and systems that must be analyzed during planning, organized during preparation, monitored and evaluated during execution, and continually assessed to protect the force from threats and hazards.

1-5. All military activities have some inherent or organic protection capability. Protection capability can be realized as complementary or reinforcing, making its application or contribution illusive to combat power generation (see FM 3-0 for more information):

- **Complementary.** Complementary capabilities protect the weakness of one system or organization with the capabilities of a different warfighting function.
- **Reinforcing.** Reinforcing capabilities combine similar systems or capabilities within the same warfighting function to increase the function's overall capabilities.

1-6. When Soldiers don a helmet or protective mask or add reactive armor to vehicles, protection is applied and existing or inherent protection is reinforced. Protection can be applied to a convoy or high-risk personnel (HRP) by surrounding them with security assets to reinforce their organic protection capacity. Physical barriers, ditches, and other tangible efforts can be applied to a base camp to reinforce or apply protection. Soldiers have vaccines applied to protect them from disease, while sensors and markings are applied to tactical vehicles to prevent fratricide.

1-7. Protection can also be realized or achieved through task organization changes that reinforce similar protection capabilities by a common purpose or by effect when dissimilar functions complement predominant protection activity. Some level of protection is achieved through complementary movement and maneuver capabilities by changing tempo, taking evasive action, or maneuvering to gain positional advantage in relation to a threat. Formations often derive protection by integrating complementary intelligence capabilities, using terrain and weather data or the cover of darkness to mask or protect movement. Some physical terrain features can offer more protection than others and are considered to complement force positioning during operational design. Protection from enemy indirect fire can be the result of reinforcing inherent survivability capabilities by dispersing command posts, while protection from enemy reconnaissance may be the result of reinforcing inherent concealment capabilities achieved from massing command posts.

1-8. Protection can be achieved from knowledge and understanding. An intelligence summary may provide Soldiers with indicators or warnings of a specific threat tactic. This knowledge may result in force preservation if actions are taken that prevent, or reduce the probability of, the success of enemy tactics. Army leaders use mission variables and assessments of environmental threats and hazards to determine when and where protection can be achieved through reinforcing action and application or through complementary effect.

OPERATIONAL ENVIRONMENT

1-9. The nature and outcome of military operations are shaped within a complex framework of environmental factors. The *operational environment* (*OE*) is defined as a composite of the conditions, circumstances, and influences that affect the employment of capabilities and bear on the decisions of the commander. (Joint Publication [JP] 3-0) (See FM 3-0 for more information.) Commanders and leaders charged with providing or ensuring protection must begin with a thorough understanding of the OE, the risks and opportunities resident there, and the ways and means available for preserving combat power through protection. Army doctrine recognizes eight operational variables (political, military, economic, social, information, infrastructure, physical environment, and time [PMESII-PT]) that can provide a foundation for a broad assessment and understanding of the OE. These operational variables can be further translated for use at the tactical level to support military operations, plans, missions, and orders through the six Army mission variables (mission, enemy, terrain and weather, troops and support available, time available, and civil considerations [METT-TC]). Using the METT-TC factors, leaders examine the environment as it relates to their mission and begin the process of identifying threats and hazards.

THREATS AND HAZARDS

1-10. The protection warfighting function preserves the combat power potential and survivability of the force by providing protection from threats and hazards.

THREATS

1-11. Threats are nation states, organizations, people, groups, conditions, or natural phenomena able to damage or destroy life, vital resources, or institutions. (See FM 3-0 for more information.) Commanders focus on threats to military operations that are generally coercive activities or information deliberately conducted or implemented by an adaptable enemy or a willful threat. Army doctrine describes threats through a range of four major categories or challenges—irregular, catastrophic, traditional, and disruptive. (See FM 3-0 for more information.) These categories can be used to begin threat identification and analysis; enhance situational understanding; and support plans, operations, and orders. (See figure 1-2, page 1-4.) Both threats and hazards have the potential to decrease combat power and the operational effectiveness of the force. For this reason, their overall assessment and mitigation is accomplished through the CRM process and applied throughout the operations process. Commanders develop risk reduction measures and controls and threat mitigation strategies for all phases of military operations and activities.

LIKELIHOOD

IRREGULAR
Guerilla Forces

- Escalates gradually
- Seeks to erode U.S. power
- Protracts the struggle
- Relies on sanctuaries
- Employs close combat

Radical Fundamentalists

Transnational Terrorists

CATASTROPHIC
Hostile Nations and Rogue States

- Seeks to paralyze U.S. forces
- Uses WMD threat as a deterrent
- Seeks to match WMD and delivery capabilities
- Requires strategic deterrence

Actors Developing WMD Capability

TRADITIONAL
Uniformed Military Forces

- Seeks to challenge U.S. power
- Employs modern conventional equipment
- Executes developed antiaccess strategy
- Avoids U.S. strength
- Exploits U.S. vulnerabilities
- Includes small-scale to theater war

Regional Adversaries

DISRUPTIVE
Other Adversaries

- Seeks to avoid conflict with the United States
- Directs actions against regional threats or rivals
- Seeks to marginalize U.S. power
- Employs latest or niche technologies
- Avoids U.S. strengths
- Exploits U.S. vulnerabilities

VULNERABILITY

Figure 1-2. Security environment

HAZARDS

1-12. *Hazard* is a condition with the potential to cause injury, illness, or death to personnel; damage to or loss of equipment or property; or mission degradation. (JP 3-33) (See FM 5-19 for more information.) Army risk management doctrine provides six categories (activity, disrupters, terrain and weather, people, time available, and legal factors) to further focus METT-TC analysis for hazard identification. (See figure 1-3.) Accidental hazards are usually predictable and preventable and can be reduced through effective risk management efforts. Commanders differentiate hazards from threats and develop focused protection strategies and priorities that match protection capabilities with the corresponding threat or hazard while synchronizing those efforts in space and time. However, hazards can be enabled by the tempo or friction or by the complacency that sometimes develops during extended military operations.

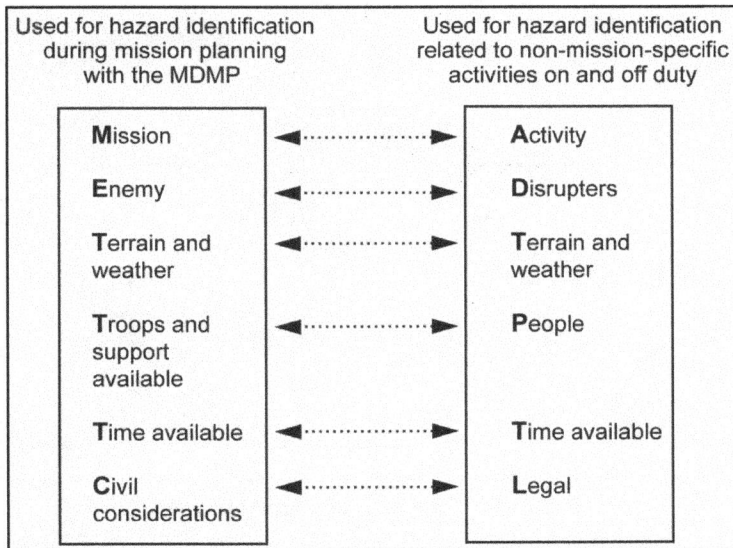

Used for hazard identification during mission planning with the MDMP		Used for hazard identification related to non-mission-specific activities on and off duty
Mission	◄·········►	Activity
Enemy	◄·········►	Disrupters
Terrain and weather	◄·········►	Terrain and weather
Troops and support available	◄·········►	People
Time available	◄·········►	Time available
Civil considerations	◄·········►	Legal

Figure 1-3. METT-TC and hazard assessment factors

COMBAT POWER

1-13. *Combat power* is the total means of destructive, constructive, and information capabilities that a military unit or formation can apply at a given time. Army forces generate combat power by converting potential into effective action. (FM 3-0) (See FM 3-0 for more information.) Combat power is generated by transforming potential into effective action that is accomplished as leaders use information to organize, integrate, and focus specific movement and maneuver, intelligence, fires, sustainment, C2, and protection capabilities to form combined arms operations. (See figure 1-4, page 1-6.) *Combined arms* is the synchronized and simultaneous application of the elements of combat power to achieve an effect greater than if each element were used separately or sequentially. (FM 3-0)

1-14. Combat power cannot be exactly quantified, and its measure leads to relative combat power analysis and assessments at best. Tactical information systems and controls measure and monitor the relative combat power potential through established running estimates and measures of effectiveness (MOEs) or measures of performance (MOPs) to provide the context for power accumulation and expenditure. Leaders interpret and use the information to provide the purpose, direction, and motivation that is necessary to focus the operation and accomplish the mission.

1-15. As an element of combat power, protection represents potential that reflects the totality of protective means in a given situation. Protection potential is not absolute and, therefore, has a latent quality that depends on leadership, mission prioritization, and resource allocation as its catalyst. Mission prioritization is simply tangible commodities and time. Protection potential can be maximized by integrating the other five elements of combat power with leadership and information to reinforce protection or to achieve complementary protective effects. The goal of protection integration at the tactical level is to balance protection potential with the freedom of action throughout the duration of military operations. This is accomplished by incrementally integrating reinforcing or complementary protection capabilities into operations until all significant vulnerabilities have been mitigated or eliminated.

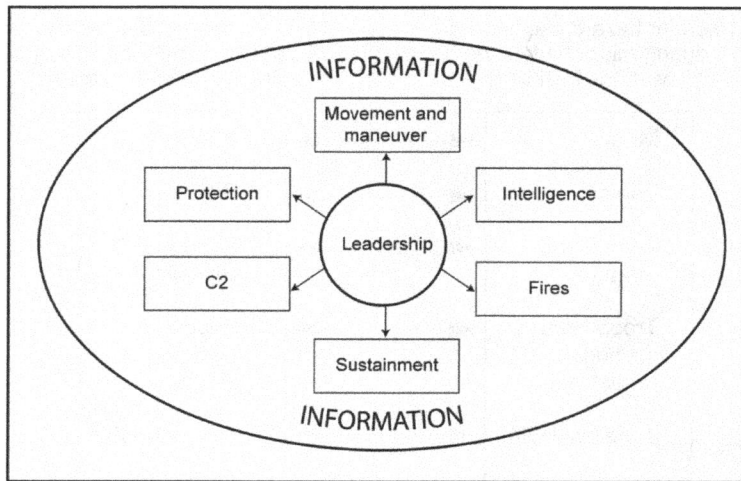

Figure 1-4. Elements of combat power

FORMS OF PROTECTION

1-16. Protection can take many forms. Military operations recognize five broad forms of protection (deterrence, prevention, active security, passive defense, and mitigation) to help organize the protection element of combat power. (See figure 1-5.) These forms of protection support battle command and the leader's visualization to provide a context within which all protection activities can be understood and further described. They are nonsequential, reflect the continuous nature of protection, and may serve as a method to conceptualize protection capabilities for conducting operations. Some military activities may support more than one form of protection at a time in an overlapping manner, reflecting the dual nature of protection as an element of combat power and as a warfighting function. Unlike maneuver, the forms of protection may orient on the terrain, the protected asset, and/or the enemy.

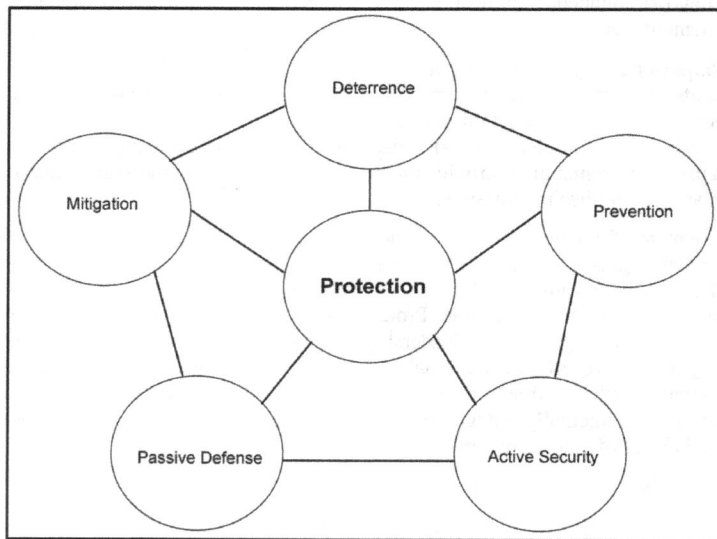

Figure 1-5. Forms of protection

DETERRENCE

1-17. The posture of an individual, formation, or structure can have a deterrent effect on threat decisionmaking and result in protection. The presence of well-trained, equipped, disciplined troops can often deter confrontation or conflict and protect the success of an operation or organization. Well-armed vehicles and fortifications may also deter enemy action and provide some level of protection for occupants and inhabitants. Random AT measures help deter terrorist attacks by disrupting routine patterns and presenting the appearance of greater security.

PREVENTION

1-18. Prevention involves the ability to neutralize, forestall, or reduce the likelihood of an imminent attack before it occurs; it can be achieved through deliberate action or as an effect. When linked to effective action, information sharing can increase situational awareness and increase protection. AT, OPSEC, and information security programs rely on situational awareness and individual protective measures to reduce the likelihood of an accident or attack. Alert and warning systems can reduce the effectiveness of an attack or environmental event. Prevention does not typically represent an offensive, preemptive capability, but may employ other measures (information engagement, civil and public affairs, preventive medicine).

ACTIVE SECURITY

1-19. Dynamic activities with the organic ability to detect, interdict, avert, disrupt, neutralize, or destroy threats and hazards while maintaining the freedom of action can provide protection to the overall operation or force. Aggressive patrolling, route security, or local security measures in the vicinity of critical assets and bases provide protection. Some air missile defense assets represent active security measures.

PASSIVE DEFENSE

1-20. Protection can be achieved from survivability positions, fortifications, and physical barriers that are designed to protect forces and material from identified threats and hazards. Some level of protection can also be derived from the geographic positioning of a formation or critical asset; this may often be the most expedient method of providing protection for some assets or resources. Bases, base clusters, tactical command posts, refuel-on-the-move positions, forward logistics elements, and detainee holding areas are all positioned after considering the protection potential of a particular location. The proximity to threats and hazards, exploitable terrain and water features, and infrastructures can contribute to combat power potential by influencing the protection potential of a specific area. The use of camouflage or smoke provides protection through passive means.

MITIGATION

1-21. Mitigation is the activities and efforts that—
* Have the ability to minimize the effects or manage the consequence of attacks and designated emergencies on personnel, physical assets, or information.
* Preserve the potential, capacity, or utility of a force or capability.
* Have a protective quality.

CBRN decontamination and PR, AT, and consequence management efforts may provide protection through mitigation and enable the restoration of essential capabilities.

PRINCIPLES OF PROTECTION

1-22. The five principles of protection—full-dimension, integrated, layered, redundant, and enduring—represent or summarize the characteristics of successful protection integration and practice. These principles provide military professionals with a context for implementing protection efforts, developing protection strategies, and allocating resources. They are not a checklist and may not apply the same way in every situation. (See figure 1-6, page 1-8.)

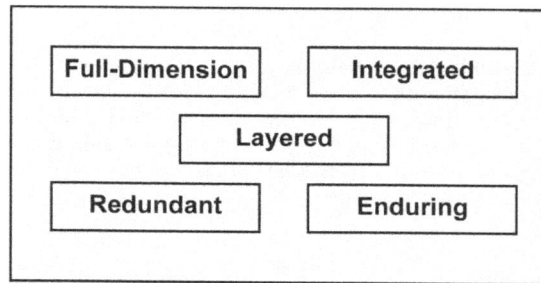

Figure 1-6. Principles of protection

FULL-DIMENSION

1-23. Protection is not a linear activity—it is a continuing and enduring activity. Protection efforts and activities must consider and account for threats and hazards in all directions, at all times, and in all environments. Protection planning, coordination, and implementation from home camp or station to an area of operations (AO) occur anywhere Soldiers or national interests are located. (See appendix A.) Situational awareness supports this principle and leads to an informed protection response.

INTEGRATED

1-24. Protection is integrated with all other activities, systems, efforts, and capabilities associated with military operations to provide strength and structure to the overall protection effort. Integration must occur vertically and horizontally in all phases of the operations process. Protection integration should complement other warfighting functions without significantly inhibiting the potential of combat power. Protection is typically integrated through various forcing functions such as working groups, meetings, and boards. (See chapter 5 for further information.)

LAYERED

1-25. Protection capabilities should be arranged using a layered approach to provide strength and depth to the overall protection system. Layering also reduces the destructive effect of a threat or hazard through the dissipation of energy or the culmination of force and may provide time to focus identification, assessment, target acquisition, or response efforts and actions. Exclusion areas, barriers, sally ports, passwords, and identity badges are examples of layering tactics, techniques, and procedures (TTP) and resources for protection.

REDUNDANT

1-26. Redundancy ensures that specific activities, systems, efforts, and capabilities critical for the success of the overall protection effort have a secondary or auxiliary effort of equal or greater capability. Redundant capabilities are not merely duplicative; they emphasize the overlapping of capabilities so that there are no seams in the protective posture. Redundancy may not be achieved in all protection measures, making it necessary to identify the critical point of failure or the critical path associated with each major protection activity, system, effort, and capability to ensure that redundancy is applied. Protection efforts are often redundant and overlapping anywhere vulnerability, weakness, or failure is identified or expected. Power generation systems, water purification systems, and patrol distribution patterns are often resourced for redundancy.

ENDURING

1-27. Protection has an enduring quality that differentiates it from defense and specific security operations. Whereas a tactical force defends only until it can resume the offense and a formation provides security in a manner that maintains freedom of action, protection has a persistent character that serves one dominant purpose—the preservation of the protected asset or capability. The enduring character of protection may affect freedom of action and resource allocation.

WARFIGHTING FUNCTIONS

1-28. Protection is one of the six warfighting functions. (See figure 1-7.) A *warfighting function* is a group of tasks and systems (people, organizations, information, and processes), united by a common purpose, that commanders use to accomplish missions and training objectives. (FM 3-0) Commanders understand, visualize, describe, and direct operations in terms of the warfighting functions as they represent tangible tasks that become plans, orders, and missions. Commanders integrate the warfighting functions to generate combat power and achieve its full destructive, disruptive, informational, or constructive potential through combined arms. Combined arms use information and the capabilities of each warfighting function in a complementary and/or reinforcing relationship with other warfighting functions. Protection is not a linear function; it is a continuing activity that can be sequentially planned but its execution and assessment are continual.

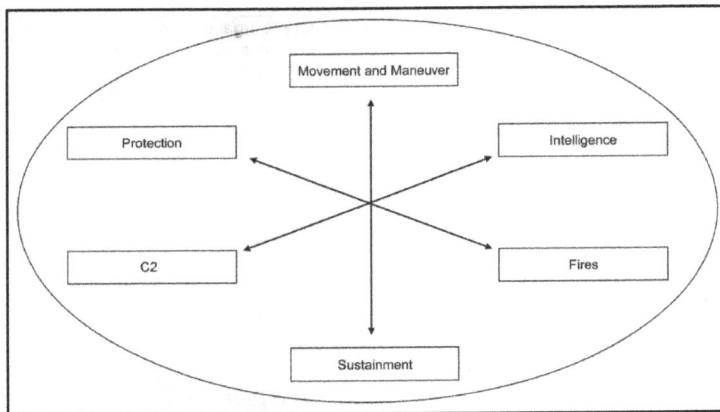

Figure 1-7. Warfighting functions

PROTECTION WARFIGHTING FUNCTION

1-29. The *protection warfighting function* is the related tasks and systems that preserve the force so the commander can apply maximum combat power. (FM 3-0) Preserving the force includes protecting personnel (combatants and noncombatants), physical assets, and information of the United States and multinational military and civilian partners. The protection warfighting function facilitates the commander's ability to maintain force integrity and combat power. Protection determines the degree to which potential threats can disrupt operations and counters or mitigates those threats.

1-30. Whereas protection as an element of combat power represents protection potential with an infinite character, the protection warfighting function serves to focus protection efforts on twelve specific tasks or systems:

- AMD.
- PR.
- Information protection.
- Fratricide avoidance.
- Operational area security.
- AT.
- Survivability.
- FHP.

- CBRN operations.
- Safety.
- OPSEC.
- EOD.

1-31. At a minimum, commanders consider the fundamentals of each task during military operations to ensure the timely integration of proper protection efforts that are necessary in time and space to preserve the force while supporting decisive, shaping, or sustaining operations. (See table 1-1.) (See chapter 2 for more information on these tasks and systems.)

Table 1-1. Protection tasks and corresponding significant activities

Protection Task	Significant Activities
AMD (FM 44-100)	**Employment Principles** • Mass. • Mix. • Mobility. • Integration.
PR (FM 3-50.1)	• Establish PR organization. • Perform cross-staff coordination. • Analyze PR gap. • Integrate diplomatic/military/civil PR. • Establish PR SOPs. • Exercise/rehearse. • Report. • Locate. • Support. • Recover. • Return/reintegrate.
Information protection (FM 3-13)	• Protect against threat events. • Monitor/detect threat events. • Analyze threat events. • Respond to threat events.
Fratricide avoidance (FM 3-90)	• Identify battlefield hazards. • Verify equipment markings. • Conduct reconnaissance. • Analyze sectors of fire. • Employ ROE. • Implement fire and maneuver control measures. • Track battlefield effects. • Rehearse.
Operational area security (FM 3-90, Appendix E)	• Conduct ISR. • Control movement. • Prepare response forces. • Employ passive defense measures. • Position sniper teams. • Defend against attacks by fire. • Support area damage control.
AT (AR 525-13)	• Establish AT program. • Collect, analyze, and disseminate threat information. • Assess and reduce critical vulnerabilities. • Plan response to terrorist threat/incident. • Increase AT awareness. • Maintain installation defense according to FPCON. • Establish civil/military partnership for WMD crises. • Conduct exercises and evaluate/assess AT plans.
Survivability (FM 5-103)	• Achieve situational awareness. • Determine degree of acceptable risk. • Analyze terrain features. • Establish priorities of work. • Employ camouflage, cover, and concealment.

Table 1-1. Protection tasks and corresponding significant activities (continued)

Protection Task	Significant Activities
FHP (FM 4-02.17)	• Prevent and control diseases. • Assess environmental and occupational health. • Determine force health activities protection. • Employ PVNTMED toxicology and laboratory services. • Perform health risk assessments. • Disseminate health information.
CBRN operations (FM 3-11, FM 3-11.21, and FM 4-02.7)	• Identify threat. • Assess situation. • Identify vulnerability reduction measures. • Conduct operations. • Provide logistics and health support. • Decontaminate.
Safety (AR 385-10; DA Pamphlet 385-10, Appendix J)	• Manage safety and occupational health program. • Investigate mishaps and near misses. • Conduct hazard analysis and recommend countermeasures. • Provide safety education, training, and promotion. • Conduct inspections, surveys, assessments, and technical consultations.
OPSEC (AR 530-1)	• Identify EEFI. • Analyze adversaries and vulnerabilities. • Assess risk. • Recommend countermeasures.
EOD (FM 4-30.51)	• Advise commanders on EO/IEDs (including CBRN). • Positively identify, respond to, and dispose of EO/IEDs (including CBRN). • Perform EO/IED site exploitation and technical intelligence collection. • Perform postblast analysis.

COMPOSITE RISK MANAGEMENT

1-32. Army leaders take prudent risks and make risk decisions on the basis of informed judgment and intuition. Risk is a function of the probability of an event occurring and the severity of the event expressed in terms of the degree to which the incident impacts combat power or mission capability. CRM is the Army's primary decisionmaking process for identifying hazards and controlling risks across the full spectrum of Army missions, functions, operations, and activities. (See FM 5-19 for more information.) CRM is a five-step process that also serves as an integrating process for the protection warfighting function in Army operations. (See figure 1-8, page 1-12.) The CRM process subjectively quantifies probability and severity through the use of the Army risk assessment matrix, leading to a determination of the risk level. (See table 1-2, page 1-12.) Risk levels help show relative significance and serve to alert and inform leaders as they make decisions regarding the course of action (COA) selection and resource allocation. CRM also helps leader decide where and when to apply protection assets and information.

1-33. The CRM process provides a general framework for identifying and reducing risks and is often supported by other, more specific tools, expertise, and processes for use in assessment and execution.

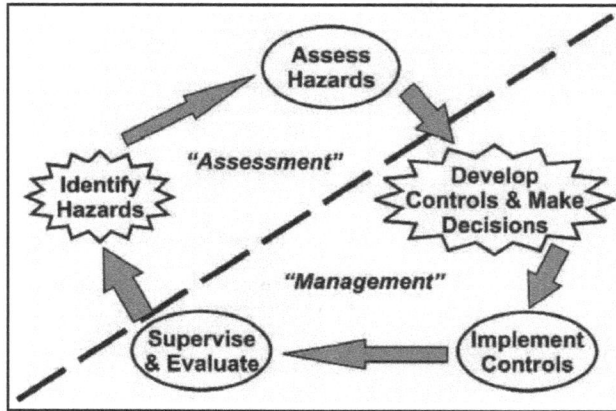

Figure 1-8. CRM process

Table 1-2. Army risk assessment matrix

Severity		Probability				
		Frequent A	Likely B	Occasional C	Seldom D	Unlikely E
Catastrophic	I	E	E	H	H	M
Critical	II	E	H	H	M	L
Marginal	III	H	M	M	L	L
Neglig ble	IV	M	L	L	L	L
E—Extremely high		H—High		M—Moderate		L—Low

Chapter 2

Protection Warfighting Function

Army operations and missions are built around tactical tasks. While protection is broadly conceptualized as an element of combat power, the protection warfighting function narrows the focus of protection to specific Army tasks. This chapter examines the twelve tasks and systems that comprise the Army protection warfighting function. FM 3-0 identifies these tasks as AMD, PR, information protection, fratricide avoidance, operational area security, AT, survivability, FHP, CBRN operations, safety, OPSEC, and EOD.

PROTECTION TASKS AND SYSTEMS

2-1.   Military operations are inherently complex. Commanders must deliberately plan and integrate the application of military force against an enemy while protecting the force and preserving combat power. The OE requires a capability-based approach to mission accomplishment. Operational and functional concepts are translated through the warfighting functions into tasks and systems for the development of plans, orders and, ultimately, unit missions. Commanders develop protection strategies for each phase of an operation or major activity. They integrate and synchronize protection tasks and systems to reduce risk, mitigate identified vulnerabilities, and act on opportunity. When properly integrated and synchronized, the tasks and systems that comprise the protection warfighting function effectively protect the force, enhance the preservation of combat power, and increase the probability of mission success.

2-2.   Units must consider the twelve protection tasks and systems and apply them as appropriate. Each task and its associated system are typically associated with a staff or staff proponent that performs specific duties.

AIR AND MISSILE DEFENSE

2-3.   An air defense system protects the force from air and missile attacks and aerial surveillance. Additionally, maneuver and fires elements in the OE must be prepared to augment air defense systems using direct-fire weapons. AMD elements protect installations and personnel from over-the-horizon strikes by conventional and weapons of mass destruction (WMD) warheads according to METT-TC. Army ground-based systems include the Phased Array Tracking Radar to Intercept of Target (PATRIOT); Avenger short-range, air defense systems; Stinger; and Norwegian Advanced, Surface-to-Air Missile System (NASAMS). Army AMD capabilities increase airspace situational awareness and complement the area air defense commander.

2-4.   Indirect-fire protection systems protect forces from threats that are largely immune to air defense artillery systems. The indirect-fire protection intercept capability is designed to detect and destroy incoming rocket, artillery, and mortar fires. This capability assesses the threat to maintain friendly protection and destroys the incoming projectile at a safe distance from the intended target.

2-5.   The AMD task consists of active and passive measures that protect personnel and physical assets from an air or missile attack. Passive measures include camouflage, cover, concealment, hardening, and OPSEC. Active measures are taken to destroy, neutralize, or reduce the effectiveness of hostile air and missile threats.

2-6.   When designing AMD protective systems, protection planners use the six employment guidelines—mutual support, overlapping fires, balanced fires, weighted coverage, early engagement, and defense in depth—and additional considerations necessary to mass and mix AMD capabilities. These employment guidelines enable air defense artillery forces to successfully accomplish combat missions and support overall force objectives. (See FM 44-100 for more information.)

AIR DEFENSE WARNING SYSTEM

2-7. The Air Defense Warning (ADW) System is an established Army system used to disseminate the probability of an air attack, air intrusion, or insertion by air into the AO. The ADW System is routinely used by ground-based air defense commanders at all levels, but can be used by all commanders to protect their forces through advanced warning. The ADW System provides collated data that can be quickly understood, facilitating a rapid response. For this reason, the ADW System is not normally tied to any other alert status or tactical warning procedure. Army doctrine recognizes the following ADWs:

- **RED.** ADW RED warns that an attack by hostile aircraft or missiles is imminent or in progress. This means that hostile aircraft or missiles are within a respective AO or that they are in the immediate vicinity of a respective AO with a high probability of entry.
- **YELLOW.** ADW YELLOW warns that an attack by hostile aircraft or missiles is probable. This means that hostile aircraft or missiles are en route toward a respective AO or that unknown aircraft or missiles suspected to be hostile are en route toward, or are within, a respective AO.
- **WHITE.** ADW WHITE warns that an attack by hostile aircraft or missiles is improbable. ADW white can be declared before or after ADW YELLOW or RED.

2-8. The ADW System is one of many tools commanders can use to rapidly influence the readiness posture of their forces in response to the probability of hostile action.

WEAPON CONTROL STATUS

2-9. *Weapon control status* describes the relative degree of control of air defense fires. (FM 44-100) Weapon control statuses can apply to weapon systems, volumes of airspace, or types of air platforms. The tactical situation normally determines the degree or extent of control necessary over particular weapon systems. AMD coordinators typically establish or recommend separate weapon control statuses for various air threats, including fixed- and rotary-wing aircraft, missiles, or unmanned aircraft systems. Air defense is optimized when all forces have the ability to rapidly receive and disseminate weapon control statuses for all air platforms. The three weapon control statuses are—

- **Weapons-free.** Fire at any air target that is not positively identified as friendly. This is the least restrictive weapon control status.
- **Weapons-tight.** Fire only at air targets positively identified as hostile according to the prevailing hostile criteria. Positive identification can be determined by a number of means (including aided or unaided visual identification) or by other designated hostile criteria (including radar identification and information network identification).
- **Weapons-hold.** Do not fire except in self-defense or in response to a formal order. This is the most restrictive weapon control status.

2-10. Any unit can receive urgent or flash message traffic in the form of a directed warning or alert of an immediate or possible threat to the force or in a specific area of the battlefield. The AMD cell provides the AMD plan to the airspace command and control (AC2) cell for integration into the corps/division unit airspace plan. Although the AC2 cell reviews and deconflicts the corps/division air defense plan with other division control measures, the control measures for the air defense plan are normally sent to higher headquarters through AMD channels. The AC2 and AMD sections must ensure that the division standing operating procedure (SOP) and respective annexes address the procedures for forwarding air defense and air control measures.

Note. See appendix B for more information on AMD and airspace management.

PERSONNEL RECOVERY

2-11. *PR* is the sum of military, diplomatic, and civil efforts to prepare for and execute the recovery and reintegration of isolated personnel. (JP 3-50) PR is the overarching term for operations that focuses on recovering isolated or missing personnel before becoming detained or captured and extracting those detained or captured personnel through coordinated and well-planned operations.

2-12. PR operations occur within a complex framework of environmental factors that shape their nature and affect their outcomes. Commanders must understand the OE and the impact of PMESII-PT to ensure that PR is incorporated into and supports each mission. This includes the characteristics of the particular OE to each mission and how aspects of the environment become essential elements in shaping the way Army forces conduct operations. Threats to isolated Soldiers will vary significantly across the spectrum of conflict.

2-13. PR is not a separate mission; it is incorporated into planning for all missions. PR guidance must synchronize the actions of commanders and staffs, recovery forces, and isolated individuals. In order to synchronize the actions of all three, commanders develop PR guidance based on command capabilities to conduct recovery operations. By knowing what actions they have dictated to potential isolated Soldiers, commanders develop situational understanding and provide guidance to their staffs and recovery forces to synchronize their actions with those of isolated Soldiers.

2-14. Commanders must integrate PR throughout the full spectrum of operations. This requires understanding the complex, dynamic relationships among friendly forces, enemies, and the environment (including the populace). This understanding helps commanders visualize and describe their intent for PR and develop focused planning guidance. As commanders develop PR guidance for subordinate units, they must ensure that subordinates have adequate combat power for PR. Commanders must also provide resources and define command relationships with the requisite flexibility to plan and execute PR operations.

2-15. Commanders provide PR planning guidance within their initial intent statement. PR planning guidance conveys the essence of the commander's visualization with respect to incorporating PR into mission planning. PR guidance provides a framework for how the unit and subordinates will synchronize the actions of isolated personnel and the recovery force. Effective PR planning guidance accounts for the OE and the continuum of operations. PR guidance is addressed in the synchronization of each warfighting function. It broadly describes how the commander intends to employ combat power to accomplish PR execution tasks within the higher commander's intent.

CORPS AND DIVISION

2-16. At corps and division levels, commanders nest PR planning variables within mission analysis and provide subordinates with PR guidance during the orders process. PR guidance allocates resources and authority to subordinate commanders, defines an overarching concept for planning and execution, and describes specific PR control measures within the overall concept. PR guidance should address available joint/interagency PR assets, procedures for coordinating those assets, and reporting procedures/requirements of PR-specific commander's critical information requirements (CCIR).

BRIGADE/GROUP AND BELOW

2-17. At brigade/group level and below, commanders refine the PR guidance from higher headquarters as it pertains to their directed mission and specific AO. This refinement results in a greater level of specificity manifested in the orders process.

BATTALION AND COMPANY

2-18. At battalion and company levels, PR guidance becomes isolated Soldier guidance (ISG). ISG is a specific directive to individual Soldiers that defines what events constitute being "isolated" and what actions to take during an isolating event. Such PR guidance is refined at battalion level, further refined at company level, and issued to Soldiers as mission-specific ISG. Samples of information to be incorporated into ISG are—

- **Definition of "isolation."** ISG should clearly tell the Soldier under what circumstances he should execute the ISG.
- **Where to go.** ISG must consider numerous factors, such as the scheme of maneuver (for the directed mission), friendly situation, enemy situation, preestablished and higher C2 measures, and battlefield control measures. Rally points may be designated in the higher order or established in the unit order. Rally points may be established specifically for the PR purpose or may be generic rally points that can serve several purposes. The "where to go" aspect may be accomplished by directing Soldiers to move in a general direction until they reach a "lateral" rally point, such as a road or river.
- **What to do.** ISG should describe actions that isolated Soldiers take, from initiating the ISG to arriving at the designated location, including actions en route to the location. The ISG should define actions (friendly and hostile) or the lack of actions that facilitate changes from the primary location and may provide alternate, contingency, and emergency locations. Security considerations that may have a bearing on friendly and hostile actions should also be addressed.
- **Signals.** This guidance can pertain to individual actions from the initiation of the ISG through the linkup with a recovery force. It covers equipment that has been issued to the Soldier and incorporates other data from paragraph 5 (Command and Control) of the unit order. It can include procedures for linking up with a recovery force and specific instructions on using a challenge and password, radios and beacons, and visual signals to overhead platforms.

2-19. Civil efforts to recover personnel or isolated persons may include sanctioned or unsanctioned intervention by intergovernmental organizations, nongovernmental organizations (NGOs), influential persons, or private citizens. Sometimes, civil organizations act independently without the knowledge of the U.S. military or government.

2-20. Diplomatic and civil PR options can be requested or can be imposed upon the senior defense representative and are most common when the isolated person has been captured or detained. (See JP 3-50 for more information.)

2-21. The ability of the Army to meet PR responsibilities hinges on leaders at every level preparing for the recovery of isolated, missing, detained, or captured personnel. Leaders must integrate PR into ongoing planning, preparation, and execution activities and consider many options for successful execution. Reintegration must be planned, giving the operator knowledge that he and his family will be taken care of during the entire PR process.

INFORMATION PROTECTION

2-22. *Information protection* is active or passive measures that protect and defend friendly information and information systems to ensure timely, accurate, and relevant friendly information. It denies enemies, adversaries, and others the opportunity to exploit friendly information and information systems for their own purposes. (FM 3-0) When pursuing their objectives, adversaries attempt to keep commanders from exercising effective C2 and, therefore, often target key decision makers and C2 information systems. Information systems are typically vulnerable along the following primary attack vectors:

- Unauthorized access.
- Malicious software.
- Electromagnetic deception.
- Electronic attack.
- Physical destruction.
- Propaganda.

2-23. Protecting information is an enduring requirement that occurs in all environments. Information protection is accomplished with a full range of protective means. Passive information protection measures are those technical and nontechnical measures that are inherent to everyday operations and directly impact users. They are designed to conceal information from, and deny information to, the threat; protect information from unauthorized modification; and protect information from unauthorized destruction. Measures include, but are not limited to, the implementation of access controls, application security, physical security, security education, communications security, and network security. Passive measures are readily standardized in unit policies and procedures.

2-24. Although carefully designated and implemented, passive protection measures reduce risk; they do not provide total protection. In order to enhance the Army's ability to safeguard information and information systems against increased threats, vulnerabilities, and attacks, protection in a dynamic network environment requires an active operational component at all echelons. Active processes consist of proactive measures that enable an organization to protect against, and counteract the dynamic nature of, a threat by using known TTPs to detect friendly vulnerabilities before the adversary. Additionally, active processes enable a unit to react decisively during an incident and recover quickly after an incident.

2-25. External and internal information perimeter protection prevents unknown or unauthorized users or data from entering a network. External efforts include communications security, router filtering, access control lists, and security guards. Where necessary, units physically isolate or place barriers between protected and unprotected networks. Internal perimeter protection consists of firewalls and router filters to serve as barriers between echelons or functional communities.

INFORMATION OPERATIONS CONDITION SYSTEM

2-26. The assistant chief of staff, signal (G-6) executes the information protection mission. The G-6 cell includes system administrators, information assurance managers, network managers, communications security personnel, and network planners. The assistant chief of staff, intelligence (G-2) provides information and intelligence regarding threats to Army information and information systems.

2-27. The G-6 disseminates the information operations condition (INFOCON), which includes electronic protection measures to units and staffs. The INFOCON demonstrates prevention through an integrated, coordinated, and structured approach to defense against and reaction to attacks on computers, networks, and information systems. (See FM 3-36 for more information.) The following INFOCON levels define preestablished, directed defensive postures designed to mitigate risks:

- **INFOCON 1.** Maximum readiness procedures.
- **INFOCON 2.** Greater readiness procedures.
- **INFOCON 3.** Enhanced readiness procedures.
- **INFOCON 4.** Increased military vigilance procedures.
- **INFOCON 5.** Network operations (NETOPS) procedures according to strategic command directive.

INFORMATION PROTECTION STRATEGIES

2-28. Information protection strategies are developed among three information protection elements—computer electronic protection, network defense, and information assurance. They protect the force from the enemy's attempts to attack friendly C2 information systems. (See FM 3-36 and FM 6-20.10 for more information.)

Nonlethal Electronic Protection

2-29. *Electronic protection* is that division of electronic warfare involving actions taken to protect personnel, facilities, and equipment from any effects of friendly or enemy use of the electromagnetic spectrum that degrade, neutralize, or destroy friendly combat capability. (JP 3-13.1) Examples of electronic protection include spectrum management, emission control procedures, hardening of equipment from electromagnetic effects, and the use of wartime reserve modes.

2-30. During operations, electronic protection includes, but is not limited to, the application of electromagnetic spectrum operations tools and associated TTP for countering enemy electronic attacks. Army forces must understand the threat and vulnerability of friendly electronic equipment to enemy electronic attack capabilities and take appropriate actions to safeguard friendly combat capability from exploitation and attack. To be successful, electronic protection must minimize the enemy's ability to conduct electronic warfare support and electronic attack operations against friendly forces.

Computer Network Defense

2-31. *Computer network defense* (CND) includes actions taken to protect, monitor, analyze, detect, and respond to unauthorized activity within Department of Defense (DOD) information systems and computer networks. (JP 6-0) It includes all measures to detect unauthorized network activity and adversary computer network attacks and to defend computers and networks against such threats. CND also employs intelligence, counterintelligence, law enforcement, and other military capabilities to defend information and computer networks. CND is an operational component of information assurance and is an enabling component of computer NETOPS. CND employs information assurance capabilities to respond to unauthorized activity within information systems and computer networks in response to a CND alert or threat information. The application of CND as a subset of information assurance provides true end-to-end, defense-in-depth protection that ensures data confidentiality, integrity, and availability as well as protection against unauthorized access.

2-32. Although the G-6 has staff responsibility for CND, effective protection is achieved through the integrated efforts of communications, law enforcement, and intelligence capabilities. System administrators ensure that users follow the appropriate procedures to prevent network intrusion.

Information Assurance

2-33. *Information assurance* consists of measures that protect and defend information and information systems by ensuring their availability, integrity, authentication, confidentiality, and nonrepudiation. This includes providing for restoration of information systems by incorporating protection, detection, and reaction capabilities. (JP 3-13) These attributes consist of—

- **Availability**—timely, reliable access to information and services by authorized users. (Available information systems operate when needed.)
- **Integrity**—protection from unauthorized change including destruction.
- **Authentication**—certainty of user or receiver identification and authorization to receive specific categories of information.
- **Confidentiality**—protection from unauthorized disclosure.
- **Nonrepudiation**—proof of message receipt and sender identification so that neither can deny having processed the information.

2-34. Information assurance, along with CND, demonstrates a layered approach through defense in depth that protects DOD systems against exploitation, degradation, and the denial of service. It does this by employing vigorous protection, detection, reaction, and restoration capabilities. This incorporation allows effective defensive measures or the timely restoration of degraded networks and information systems. Information assurance defense in depth protects all networks, including their information systems, computers, radios, infrastructure implementation, gateways, routers, and switches. (See FM 3-36 and FM 6-20.10 for more information.)

FRATRICIDE AVOIDANCE

2-35. **Fratricide is the unintentional killing of friendly personnel by friendly firepower.** The destructive power and range of modern weapons, coupled with the high intensity and rapid tempo of combat, increase the potential for fratricide. Tactical maneuvers, terrain, and weather conditions may also increase the danger of fratricide.

2-36. Fratricide is accidental and is usually the end product of an error by a leader and/or Soldier. Accurate information about locations and activities of friendly and hostile forces and an aggressive airspace management plan help commanders avoid fratricide. Liaison officers increase situational understanding and enhance interoperability. Leaders and Soldiers must know the range and blast characteristics of their weapon systems and munitions to prevent ricochet, penetration, and other unintended effects.

2-37. Commanders and leaders are responsible for preventing fratricide. They must lower the probability of fratricide without discouraging boldness and audacity. Good leadership that results in positive weapons control, control of troop movements, and disciplined operational procedures contributes to achieving this goal. Situational understanding and friendly personnel and combat identification methods also help. Eliminating fratricide increases Soldier willingness to act boldly with the confidence that misdirected friendly fires will not kill them. Additionally, more host nation contractors, day laborers, and NGO personnel who support Army operations face the same risks as U.S. forces. Since these personnel work and often live in and among U.S. forces, commanders must include them in protection and combat identification plans. This may significantly increase the protection responsibility of commanders.

2-38. Commanders protect the fighting spirit of Soldiers through effective leadership and morale. Incidents of fratricide can degrade unit effectiveness and combat power potential. The loss of confidence, hesitation, oversupervision, and excessive caution are just some of the negative reactions that can afflict leaders and Soldiers following a fratricide incident.

2-39. Fratricide avoidance is normally accomplished through a protection strategy that emphasizes prevention, centered on two fundamental areas—situational awareness and target identification. Fratricide may also be more prevalent during joint and coalition operations when communications and interoperability challenges are not fully resolved.

- **Situational awareness.** *Situational awareness* is the immediate knowledge of the conditions of the operation, constrained geographically and in time. (FM 3-0) It includes the real-time, accurate knowledge of one's own location and orientation and the locations, activities, and intentions of other friendly, enemy, neutral, or noncombatant elements in the AO, sector, zone, or immediate vicinity.
- **Target identification.** *Target identification* is the accurate and timely characterization of a detected object on the battlefield as friend, neutral, enemy, or unknown. (FM 3-20.15) Unknown objects should not be engaged; rather, the target identification process continues until positive identification has been made. An exception to this is a weapons-free zone where units can fire at anything that is not positively identified as friendly.

2-40. The potential for fratricide may increase with the fluid nature of the noncontiguous battlefield and the changing disposition of attacking and defending forces. The presence of noncombatants in the AO further complicates operations. Simplicity and clarity are often more important than a complex, detailed plan when developing fratricide avoidance methods. (See appendix B for more information.)

OPERATIONAL AREA SECURITY

2-41. *Operational area security* **is a form of security operations conducted to protect friendly forces, installations, routes, and actions within an AO.** (See FM 3-90 for a detailed discussion of security operations.) Forces engaged in area security operations focus on the force, installation, route, area, or asset to be protected. Although vital to the success of military operations, area security is normally an economy-of-force mission, often designed to ensure the continued conduct of sustainment operations and to support decisive and shaping operations. (FM 7-15 provides a critical task list for area security operations.)

2-42. Area security may be the predominant method of protecting support areas that are necessary to facilitate the positioning, employment, and protection of resources required to sustain, enable, and control tactical forces. Area security operations are often emphasized in noncontiguous AOs to compensate for the lack of protection integrity that large or distant, unoccupied areas often create. Area security operations are often an effective method of providing civil security and control during some stability operations. Forces engaged in area security operations can saturate an area or position on key terrain to provide protection through early warning, reconnaissance, or surveillance and guard against unexpected enemy attack with an active response. Area security operations often focus on named area of interests in an effort to answer CCIR, aiding in tactical decisionmaking and confirming or denying threat intentions. Forces engaged in area security operations are typically organized in a manner that emphasizes their mobility, lethality, and communications capabilities. The maneuver enhancement brigade (MEB) and some military police units are specifically equipped and trained to conduct area security and may constitute the only available force during some phases of an operation. However, area security operations take advantage of the local security measures performed by all units, regardless of their location in the AO.

2-43. Commanders at all levels apportion combat power and dedicate assets to protection tasks and systems based on an analysis of the OE, the likelihood of threat action, and the relative value of friendly resources and populations. Although all resources have value, the mission variables of METT-TC make some resources, assets, or locations more significant to successful mission accomplishment from enemy and friendly perspectives. Commanders rely on the CRM process and other specific assessment methods to facilitate decisionmaking, issue guidance, and allocate resources. Criticality, vulnerability, and recuperability are some of the most significant considerations in determining protection priorities that become the subject of commander guidance and the focus of area security operations. Area security operations often focus on the following assets and activities:

- **Base and base cluster defense.** *Base defense* is the local military measures, both normal and emergency, required to nullify or reduce the effectiveness of enemy attacks on, or sabotage of, a base to ensure that the maximum capacity of its facilities is available to U.S. forces. (JP 1-02) A division or corps may be required to protect multiple forward operating bases (FOBs). Units may be assigned base defense operations on a permanent or rotating basis, depending on the mission variables.
- **Critical asset security.** *Critical asset security* **is the protection and security of personnel and physical assets and/or information analyzed and deemed essential to the operation and success of the mission and the required resources for protection.** This designation generally comes as a result of a deliberate assessment or as a directed mission.
- **C2 node protection.** Command posts and operations centers are often protected through area security techniques that involve the employment of an array of protection and security assets in a layered, integrated, and redundant manner. This can often keep hostile threats at a distance by maximizing the standoff distance from explosive effects while keeping the protected asset outside the range of enemy direct-fire weapons and observation.
- **HRP security.** *HRP* are personnel who, by their grade, assignment, symbolic value, or relative isolation, are likely to be attractive or accessible terrorist targets. (JP 3-07.2) Special precautions are taken to ensure the safety and security of these individuals and their family members. When units identify a significant risk to selected personnel, the local commander normally organizes security details from internal resources. However, under certain circumstances, designated personnel may require protective service details by specially trained units.
- **Physical security.** *Physical security* consists of that part of security concerned with physical measures designed to safeguard personnel; to prevent unauthorized access to equipment, installations, material, and documents; and to safeguard them against espionage, sabotage, damage, and theft. (JP 6-0) (See FM 3-19.30 for more information.) Physical security measures as they pertain to AT identify physical vulnerabilities to terrorist attacks of bases, personnel, and materiel and take actions to reduce or eliminate those vulnerabilities. Survivability operations and general engineering support may be required to emplace compensatory measures for identified vulnerabilities. The physical security system builds on the premise that baseline security and the preparedness posture are based on the local threat, site-specific vulnerabilities, identified critical assets, and available resources.
- **Response force operations.** Response force operations expediently reinforce a unit's organic protection capabilities or complement that protection with maneuver capabilities based on the threat. Response force operations include the planning for defeat of Level I and Level II threats and the shaping of Level III threats until a designated combined arms, tactical combat force (TCF) arrives for decisive operations. (Threat levels are discussed in appendix C.) Response force operations use a mobile force with appropriate fire support (usually designated by the area commander) to deal with Level II threats in the AO. (See FM 3-19.1 for more information.)
- **Lines of communications security.** The security and protection of lines of communications and supply routes are critical to military operations since most support traffic moves along these routes. The security of supply routes and lines of communication (rail, pipeline, highway, and waterway) presents one of the greatest security problems in an AO. Route security operations are defensive in nature and are terrain-oriented. A route security force may prevent an enemy force

from impeding, harassing, or destroying traffic along a route or portions of a route by establishing a movement corridor. (See FM 3-90.31.) Units conduct synchronized operations (reconnaissance, security, mobility, information engagement) within the movement corridor. A movement corridor may be established in a high-risk area to facilitate the movement of a single element, or it may be an enduring operation.

- **Checkpoints and combat outposts.** It is often necessary to control the freedom of movement in an AO for a specific period of time or as an enduring operation. This may be accomplished by placing permanent or temporary checkpoints and combat outposts along designated avenues and roadways or on key terrain identified through METT-TC. Checkpoints are used for controlling, regulating, and verifying movement; and combat outposts are used for sanctuary; support; information, surveillance, and reconnaissance (ISR); or area denial. (See FM 3-24.2 for more information on combat outposts.)

- **Convoy security.** *Convoy security operations* are specialized area security operations conducted to protect convoys. (FM 3-90) Units conduct convoy security operations anytime there are insufficient friendly forces to continuously secure routes in an AO and there is a significant danger of enemy ground action directed against the convoy. Commanders may also conduct convoy security operations in conjunction with route security operations. Planning includes designating units for convoy security, providing guidance on TTP for units to provide for their own security during convoys, or establishing protection and security requirements for convoys carrying critical assets. Local or theater policy typically dictates when or which convoys receive security and protection. (See FM 4-01.45 for more information on convoy security training requirements and TTP.)

- **Port area and pier security.** Ground forces may typically provide area security for port and pier areas. The joint force commander and subordinate joint force commanders ensure that port security plans and responsibilities are clearly delineated and assigned. Area commanders who are assigned a port area as part of their AO must develop and organize plans to ensure that forces are trained, led, and equipped to concentrate the necessary combat power at the decisive time and place to protect or secure port areas and cargo as necessary. The patrol of harbors and anchorages is generally the mission of a dedicated port security unit and may include waterfront security operations. (See JP 3-10 for more information on port security units.)

- **Surveillance.** *Surveillance* is the systematic observation of aerospace, surface or subsurface areas, places, persons, or things by visual, aural, electronic, photographic, or other means. (JP 3-0) (See JP 1-02 and FM 2-0 for more information.) The protection working group uses staff analysis and coordination with higher headquarters to determine which critical assets or locations are likely to be attractive targets and require surveillance.

- **Area damage control.** Commanders conduct area damage control when the damage and scope of the attack are limited and they can respond and recover with local assets and resources. Optimally, commanders aim to recover immediately. This recovery involves resuming operations, maintaining or restoring order, evacuating casualties, isolating danger or hazard areas, and mitigating personnel and materiel losses. Some attacks may rise to the level of incidents of national significance and require additional resources for mitigation, recovery, and investigation. In the latter case, commanders transition from area damage control to consequence management activities.

ANTITERRORISM

2-44. AT is the Army's defensive program to protect against terrorism. Army AT focuses on risk management, planning (including the AT plan), training, exercises, resource generation, comprehensive program review, and the conduct of random AT measures. AT planning coordinates specific AT security requirements with the efforts of other security enhancement programs, such as intelligence support to AT, law enforcement, physical security, and others. Effective AT programs synchronize intelligence, CRM, and existing security programs to provide a holistic approach to defend against terrorist threats. Units at each echelon typically have at least one qualified AT officer assigned. (See DODI 2006.16 and Army Regulation [AR] 525-13 for more information.)

> *Note.* Units at each echelon should have at least one assigned Level II AT officer.

ANTITERRORISM PROGRAMS, TASKS, AND SYSTEMS

2-45. AT is an integral part of Army efforts to defeat terrorism. Terrorists can target Army elements at any time, in any location. By effectively preventing and, if necessary, responding to terrorist attacks, commanders protect all activities and people so that Army missions can proceed unimpeded. AT is neither a discrete task nor the sole responsibility of a single branch; all bear responsibility. AT must be integrated into all Army operations and considered at all times. CONUS installations, recruiting stations, Corps of Engineers projects, and combat actions should consider AT principles in every assigned task. Awareness must be built into every mission, every Soldier, and every leader. Integrating AT represents the foundation that is crucial for Army success. Typical Army AT programs are composed of several adjunct and information programs, including the following areas at a minimum:

- Risk management (threat, critical asset, and vulnerability assessments of units, installations, facilities, and bases).
- AT planning (units, installations, facilities, and bases).
- AT awareness training and command information programs.
- Integration of various vulnerability assessments of units, installations, facilities, bases, personnel, and activities.
- AT protection measures to protect individual personnel, HRP, physical assets (physical security), designated critical assets (area security), and information.
- Resource application.
- Civil and military partnerships for domestic and foreign consequence management.
- Force protection condition (FPCON) system to support terrorist threat and incident response plans.
- Comprehensive AT program review.

2-46. Army commanders implement eight standard AT tasks to support DOD AT objectives. These objectives aim to deter incidents, employ countermeasures, mitigate effects, and conduct incident recovery. The AT tasks are—

- **Establish an AT program.** Commanders communicate the spirit and intent of all AT policies throughout the chain of command or line of authority by establishing AT programs. The programs provide standards, policies, and procedures to reduce the vulnerabilities from terrorist attacks.
- **Collect, analyze, and disseminate threat information.** Commanders develop a system to collect, analyze, and disseminate terrorist threat information and apply the appropriate FPCONs.
- **Assess and reduce critical vulnerabilities.** Commanders continuously assess AT efforts. These assessments review the overall program, individual physical and procedural security measures, and unit predeployment preparation.
- **Increase AT awareness in every Soldier, civilian, and Family member.** Commanders inform all personnel of the terrorist threat and adequately train them to apply protective measures. Unit collective training includes AT training, regardless of the unit location.
- **Maintain installation defenses according to FPCONs.** Commanders use AT-specific security procedural and physical measures to protect personnel, information, and materiel from terrorist threats.
- **Establish civil/military partnerships for a terrorist incident crisis.** Commanders coordinate with local civilian communities to establish working relationships and formulate partnerships to combat and defend against terrorism.

- **Establish terrorist threat and incident response planning.** Commanders and agency and activity heads develop reactive plans. These plans prescribe appropriate actions for reporting terrorist threat information, responding to terrorist threats and attacks, and reporting terrorist incidents.
- **Conduct exercises and evaluate and assess AT plans.** Commanders institute an exercise program that develops, refines, and tests AT response procedures to terrorist threats and incidents. This exercise program ensures that AT is an integral part of exercise planning.

FORCE PROTECTION CONDITION SYSTEM

2-47. The FPCON system standardizes DOD identification, recommended preventive actions, and responses to terrorist threats against U.S. personnel and facilities. This system is the principal means for a commander to apply an operational decision on how to protect against terrorism, and it facilitates inter-Service coordination and support for AT activities. DOD establishes the baseline FPCON levels and measures, and commanders develop site-specific measures and procedures for implementing them. Well-designed AT measures facilitates threat detection, assessment, delay, denial, and notification. FPCON measures include provisions for reinforcing physical security; increasing security personnel and inspections of vehicles, handcarried items, and packages; random AT measures; and other emergency measures. FPCON measures are designed to be scalable and proportional to changes in the local threat (See AR 525-13 for more information.) The five FPCON levels are—

- **NORMAL.** FPCON NORMAL applies when a general global threat of possible terrorist activity exists and warrants a routine security posture. At a minimum, access control will be conducted at all DOD installations and facilities.
- **ALPHA.** FPCON ALPHA applies when there is an increased general threat of possible terrorist activity against personnel or facilities, and the nature and extent of the threat are unpredictable. FPCON ALPHA measures must be capable of being maintained indefinitely.
- **BRAVO.** FPCON BRAVO applies when an increased or more predictable threat of terrorist activity exists. Sustaining FPCON BRAVO measures for a prolonged period may affect operational capability and military-civil relationships with local authorities.
- **CHARLIE.** FPCON CHARLIE applies when an incident occurs or intelligence is received that indicates some form of terrorist action or targeting against personnel or facilities is likely. The prolonged implementation of FPCON CHARLIE measures may create hardship and affect the activities of the unit and its personnel.
- **DELTA.** FPCON DELTA applies in the immediate area where a terrorist attack has occurred or when intelligence has been received that terrorist action against a specific location or person is imminent. This FPCON is usually declared as a localized condition. FPCON DELTA measures are not intended to be sustained for an extended duration.

Note. A complete list of site-specific AT security measures linked to each particular FPCON is generally contained in the installation, facility, or base AT plan.

2-48. Successful AT activities involve the overlapping of several protection tasks and systems. Incident response clarifies procedures for C2 and the actions of responders. These actions include determining the full nature and scope of the incident, containing damage, and reporting information to higher headquarters. These measures can contribute to deterring attacks if potential adversaries recognize that U.S. forces are vigilant and ready to respond to an incident. Incident response measures include emergency response, disaster planning, and preparedness to recover from a terrorist attack.

2-49. Perimeter security requires a combination of physical security measures, such as protective obstacles, physical barriers, fencing, protective lighting, and electronic security systems. Security personnel continuously observe and assess measures, access control, entry control points, and guard towers. Survivability operations help enable perimeter security by emplacing physical barriers, building survivability positions, and hardening sites.

SURVIVABILITY

2-50. *Survivability* includes all aspects of protecting personnel, weapons, and supplies while simultaneously deceiving the enemy. Survivability tactics include building a good defense; employing frequent movement; using concealment, deception, and camouflage; and constructing fighting and protective positions for both individuals and equipment. (JP 3-34)

2-51. *Survivability operations* are the development and construction of protective positions (such as earth berms, dug-in positions, overhead protection, and countersurveillance means) to reduce the effectiveness of enemy weapon systems. (FM 3-34) It also includes other mitigation TTP, such as fire prevention and firefighting. (See FM 5-415 for more information.) Survivability and survivability operations combine technology and methods that afford the maximum protection to Army forces. Survivability operations range from employing camouflage, concealment, and deception (including the supporting task of battlefield obscuration) to hardening facilities, C2 nodes, and critical infrastructure.

2-52. Survivability operations frequently enable other protection tasks and systems, including AMD, operational area security, AT, and CBRN operations. Survivability operations also provide support to the movement and maneuver warfighting function by conducting mobility and countermobility operations.

2-53. Commanders may call on engineers to support the protection efforts of combat or sustainment units. Engineers can mass their skills and equipment to develop defensive positions into fortifications or strongpoints and improve existing defensive positions. Within a missile threat environment, engineers provide field fortification support to harden key assets against missile attacks. They also provide survivability applications to host nation facilities and U.S.-operated facilities. These applications can include entry control points, guard towers, and other means of hardening. Engineers provide protective measures against terrorists that threaten U.S. forces or national interests. (See FM 5-103 for more information.)

2-54. While survivability operations are traditionally recognized as an engineer task, units at all echelons have an inherent responsibility to improve their positions, whether a fighting position, bunker, or FOB. Survivability consists of four areas that are designed to focus efforts toward mitigating friendly losses to hostile actions or environments:

- **Mobility.** Survivability of friendly forces is much more likely when they are moving or when they possess the ability to reposition quickly. Maintaining freedom of movement and repositioning often increases survivability. Static units must maintain the capability to move on short notice.
- **Situational understanding.** *Situational understanding* is the product of applying analysis and judgment to relevant information to determine the relationship among the mission variables to facilitate decisionmaking. (FM 3-0) It requires the ability to identify, process, and comprehend the critical elements of information about what occurs inside a commander's AO. Having accurate situational understanding provides the baseline for hazard assessments.

Note. The situational understanding of terrain, through proper terrain analysis, is important to survivability and the development of survivability positions, minimizing the requirements to adjust terrain and leading to the efficient use of survivability assets.

- **Hardening.** Hardening is the act of using natural or man-made materials to protect personnel, equipment, or facilities. Hardening measures protect resources from blast, direct and indirect fire, heat, radiation, or electronic warfare. Hardening is accomplished by using barriers, walls, shields, berms, or other types of physical protection. It is intended to defeat or negate the effects of an attack and includes fighting positions, protective positions, armored vehicles, Soldiers, and information systems.
- **Camouflage, concealment, and deception.** Camouflage, concealment, and deception use materials and techniques to hide, blend, disguise, decoy, or disrupt the appearance of military targets and their backgrounds to prevent visual and electronic detection of friendly forces. Camouflage, concealment, and deception help prevent an enemy from detecting or identifying

friendly troops, equipment, activities, or installations and include battlefield obscuration capabilities to obscure, screen, mark, or deceive. Battlefield obscuration is a major supporting task of camouflage, concealment, and deception and is typically provided by specialized CBRN elements or fires.

2-55. Fire prevention, fire suppression, and firefighting encompass all efforts aimed at preventing or stopping fires. Fire prevention programs exist at all levels, and all levels of command are responsible for the Army's fire protection plan. Commanders and supervisors are responsible for the fire safety policies and plans in their organizations. Army firefighting capabilities consist of general firefighting and tactical firefighting:

- **General firefighting.** General firefighting skills are embedded into all Army safety programs (annual drivers' training, unit fire safety, unit fire prevention) and during the transportation of personnel, petroleum, munitions, and explosives.
- **Tactical firefighting,** Tactical firefighting requires more specialized capabilities and is typically provided by engineer, host nation, or other identified firefighting units. In addition to normal fire protection/suppression, tactical firefighting capabilities include administering first aid; providing initial response to hazmat incidents; and rescuing entrapped, sick, and injured personnel from aircraft, buildings, equipment, vehicles, water, confined spaces, and high angles.

Note. See FM 5-415 for more information.

FORCE HEALTH PROTECTION

2-56. FHP includes measures taken by commanders, leaders, individual Soldiers, and the military health system to promote, improve, or conserve the behavioral and physical well-being of Soldiers. These measures enable a healthy and fit force, prevent injury and illness, and protect the force from health hazards. It includes the prevention aspects of several Army Medical Department functions, such as—

- Preventive medicine, including medical surveillance and occupational and environmental health surveillance.
- Veterinary services, including food safety and surety, animal care missions, and the prevention of zoonotic diseases transmissible to man.
- Combat and operational stress control.
- Laboratory services, including area medical laboratory (AML) support.
- Dental services, including preventive dentistry.

2-57. Army personnel must be physically and behaviorally fit. This requirement demands programs that promote and improve the capacity of personnel to perform military tasks at high levels, under extreme conditions, and for extended periods of time. These preventive and protective capabilities include physical exercise, nutritional diets, dental hygiene and restorative treatment, combat and operational stress management, rest, recreation, and relaxation that are geared to individual and/or organizations.

2-58. Methods to prevent disease are best applied synergistically. Sanitation practices, waste management, and pest and vector control are crucial to disease protection. Regional spraying and insect repellent application to guard against hazardous flora and fauna are examples of prevention methods. Prophylactic measures can encompass human and animal immunizations, dental chemoprophylaxis and treatment, epidemiology, optometry, counseling on specific health threats, and protective clothing and equipment.

2-59. The key to preventive and protective care is information—the capacity to anticipate the current and true health environment and its proper delivery to the affected human population. Derived from robust health surveillance and medical intelligence, this information addresses occupational, local environmental, and enemy-induced threat from industrial hazards; air and water pollution; endemic or epidemic disease; and chemical, biological, radiological, nuclear, and high-yield explosives (CBRNE); and directed energy device weapons (including high-powered microwaves, particle beams, and lasers). Health service support must be capable of acquiring, storing, moving, and providing information that is timely, relevant, accurate, concise, and applicable to the intended human user. In summary, this information capability is crucial to FHP.

PREVENTIVE MEDICINE SERVICES

2-60. Preventive medicine services are essential to maintaining and sustaining force health from garrison through deployment, to combat, and upon return to the home station. These services primarily prevent disease and nonbattle injuries from affecting Soldiers. Personnel actively monitor the AO for disease, conduct preventive services (such as immunizations and prophylaxes), and provide subject matter expert advice when Soldiers become exposed to hazards. Personnel provide assistance to control excessive occupational and environmental health exposure to hazards, such as noise, toxic industrial material (TIM), and climate extremes. Through field sanitation team training and water assessments, preventive medicine personnel educate Soldiers in disease and nonbattle injury prevention. Preventive medicine services establish medical, occupational, and environmental health screenings; connect to everything Soldiers do; and are a constant requirement regardless of the enemy threat. (See FM 4-02.17 for more information.)

Medical Surveillance

2-61. *Medical surveillance* is the ongoing, systematic collection, analysis, and interpretation of data derived from instances of medical care or medical evaluation, and the reporting of population-based information for characterizing and countering threats to a population's health, well-being, and performance. (JP 4-02) Medical surveillance is essential to planning, implementing, and evaluating public health practices. It closely integrates with the timely dissemination of data as required by higher authority. This program provides the commander a trend analysis that is vital to hazard assessment for operations in an AO.

Occupational and Environmental Health Surveillance

2-62. *Occupational and environmental health surveillance* is the regular or repeated collection, analysis, archiving, interpretation, and dissemination of occupational and environmental health-related data for monitoring the health of, or potential health hazard impact on, a population and individual personnel, and for intervening in a timely manner to prevent, treat, or control the occurrence of disease or injury when determined necessary. (JP 4-02) Occupational and environmental health surveillance is an ongoing process.

VETERINARY SERVICES

2-63. The focus of veterinary services is food and animals. It covers food safety and defense and the quality assurance of food during all stages of procurement, storage, and distribution; veterinary medical care for military working dogs; and veterinary preventive medicine. Veterinary personnel are trained to perform surveillance inspections of operational rations; and they examine and inspect food, ice, and bottled water sources for contamination. In the event of CBRN contamination, these personnel can determine whether packaged food sources are consumable. Veterinary personnel inspect all service-owned subsistence received, stored, issued, sold, or shipped from or to military installations (including those items received from depots and supply points). (See AR 40-656 for more information.)

2-64. Veterinary personnel provide complete care for military working dogs, limited care for other DOD and government-owned animals when time and resources permit, and limited care to indigenous animals as directed. The veterinary preventive medicine mission includes prevention and control programs to protect Soldiers from food-borne diseases. It establishes animal disease prevention and control programs to protect Soldiers and their families, contractors, and other personnel from zoonotic diseases. Veterinary personnel evaluate zoonotic disease data collected in the AO and advise preventive medicine elements and higher headquarters on potential hazards to humans. They also investigate unexplained animal deaths, including livestock and wildlife. (See FM 4-02.18 for more information.)

COMBAT AND OPERATIONAL STRESS CONTROL

2-65. Unit mental health sections provide combat and operational stress control for supported units. Combat and operational stress control is accomplished through vigorous prevention, consultation, training, education, and Soldier restoration programs. These programs provide behavioral health expertise to unit leaders and Soldiers where they serve to sustain their mission focus and effectiveness under heavy and prolonged stress. Mental health sections identify Soldiers with combat and operational stress reactions and those who need rest and restoration in or near their unit area for rapid return to duty. These programs aim to maximize the return-to-duty rate of Soldiers who are temporarily impaired, have a behavior health diagnosis, or have stress-related conditions. Preventing posttraumatic stress disorders is an important objective for all Army leaders. (See FM 4-02.51 for more information.)

MEDICAL LABORATORY SERVICES

2-66. Medical laboratory services are needed to support FHP activities in identifying and evaluating occupational and environmental health hazards in the AO. Services may be provided by capabilities that are organic to deployed medical treatment facilities or by separate preventive medicine and medical laboratory units like the AML. Services may include the accurate field confirmatory laboratory testing of suspect biological and chemical warfare agents, endemic and zoonotic diseases, and occupational and environmental agents.

PREVENTIVE DENTISTRY

2-67. Military preventive dentistry incorporates primary, secondary, and tertiary preventive measures taken to reduce or eliminate oral conditions that decrease Soldier fitness to perform the mission and cause absence from duty. Dental care measures for Soldiers are described under preventive dentistry and known as the Dental Combat Effectiveness Program. Before operational deployment, preventive dentistry measures include the Basic Combat Training/Advanced Individual Training Dental Program (a program to treat Class 3 dental patients), the Soldier Readiness Program (described in AR 600-8-101), and the preventive dentistry programs described in AR 40-35. (See FM 4-02.19 for more information.)

2-68. Deployed Soldiers are at higher risks of developing oral diseases, probably due to inadequate oral hygiene and altered nutritional intake. Nearly all oral disease is preventable with the use of good personal health habits (proper diet and nutrition, oral hygiene, and substance abuse). Effective oral disease prevention methods are simple, inexpensive, and readily available. During deployment, commanders must ensure that primary preventive services are implemented and monitored to improve the dental readiness of Soldiers in support of military operations. Leaders ensure that drinking water supplied to Soldiers is optimally fluoridated, when possible, and provide oral health information in the AO at every opportunity. Leaders ensure that Soldiers are aware of healthful stress reduction habits and techniques and that they know the importance of avoiding harmful oral habits, such as tobacco use and improper diet. Soldiers should have access to oral hygiene devices and have the opportunity to practice good oral hygiene. Soldiers receive dental floss, toothbrushes, and fluoridated toothpaste in the Ration Supplement, Sundries Pack, Type I. Local Post Exchanges also carry oral hygiene supplies.

CHEMICAL, BIOLOGICAL, RADIOLOGICAL, AND NUCLEAR OPERATIONS

2-69. CBRN operations are the employment of tactical capabilities that counter the entire range of CBRN threats and hazards through WMD proliferation prevention, WMD counterforce, CBRN defense, and CBRN consequence management activities in support of operational and strategic objectives to combat WMD and operate safely in CBRN environments. CBRN threats and hazards include WMD, improvised weapons and devices, and TIM and can potentially cause mass casualties and large-scale destruction. Many state and nonstate actors (including terrorists and criminals) possess or have the capability to possess, develop, or proliferate WMD. U.S. policy prohibits the use of chemical or biological weapons under any circumstances, but it reserves the right to employ nuclear weapons. Many potential enemies are under no such constraint. (See FM 3-11 for more information.)

2-70. The CBRN and EOD elements of the protection cell plan and coordinate CBRNE operations. Key capabilities also integrate with other warfighting functions. Among these, CBRN reconnaissance and surveillance integrate with the intelligence warfighting function, the CBRN warning and reporting system integrates with the command and control warfighting function, and CBRN decontamination operations support the sustainment warfighting function.

SUPPORT TO COMBATING WEAPONS OF MASS DESTRUCTION

2-71. The United States confronts the threat of CBRN threats and their means of delivery through the mutually reinforcing strategic activities of nonproliferation, counterproliferation, and consequence management. U.S. military CBRN units were once primarily defensive in nature, with heavy emphasis on response and mitigation measures. Lessons learned from Operation Iraqi Freedom and Operation Enduring Freedom have expanded this role from passive defense to tactical execution or support of the eight military mission areas to combat WMD. (See JP 3-40 for more information.)

2-72. CBRN operations in support of combating WMD include—

- **Providing WMD security cooperation and partner activities support.** WMD security cooperation and partner activities improve or promote defense relationships and the capacity of allied and partner nations to execute or support the other military mission areas to combat WMD through military-to-military contact, burden-sharing arrangements, combined military activities, and support to international activities.
- **Providing WMD threat reduction cooperation support.** WMD threat reduction cooperation activities are undertaken with the consent and cooperation of host nation authorities in a permissive environment to enhance physical security and to reduce, dismantle, redirect, and/or improve the protection of a state's existing WMD program, stockpiles, and capabilities.
- **Conducting WMD interdiction operations.** WMD interdiction operations track, intercept, search, divert, seize, or otherwise stop the transit of WMD; WMD delivery systems; or related materials, technologies, and expertise.
- **Conducting WMD offensive operations.** WMD offensive operations disrupt, neutralize, or destroy a WMD threat before it can be used or deter the subsequent use of WMD.
- **Conducting WMD elimination operations.** WMD elimination operations are conducted in a hostile or uncertain environment to systematically locate, characterize, secure, disable, or destroy WMD programs and related capabilities. (See Field Manual Interim [FMI] 3-90.10 for more information.)
- **Conducting CBRN active defense.** CBRN active defense includes measures to defeat an attack with CBRN weapons by employing actions to divert, neutralize, or destroy those weapons or their means of delivery while en route to their target.
- **Conducting CBRN passive defense.** CBRN passive defense includes measures taken to minimize or negate the vulnerability to, and effects of, CBRN attacks. This mission area focuses on maintaining force ability to continue military operations in a CBRN environment. Commanders use measures that implement the principles of contamination avoidance (see FM 3-11.3), protection (see FM 3-11.4), and decontamination (see FM 3-11.5).
- **Conducting CBRN consequence management operations.** CBRN consequence management includes activities that are undertaken, when directed or authorized, to mitigate the deliberate or inadvertent release of CBRN hazards. (See FM 3-11.21 for more information.)

MISSION-ORIENTED PROTECTIVE POSTURE ANALYSIS

2-73. Protecting Soldiers from the harmful hazards associated with CBRN attacks in an AO is essential to preserving combat power. When the probability of CBRN threat exists, commanders and leaders must conduct a deliberate analysis to posture and equip forces for survival and mission effectiveness. CBRN and medical personnel consider METT-TC and related information to provide recommendations on protection requirements that are reflected in the mission-oriented protective posture (MOPP) level. Staff and leader involvement is necessary to ensure safe and sustained operations under various climatic conditions. Commanders should develop standard responses and COAs for each projected mission. The standard MOPP levels are—

- **MOPP Ready.** Carry a protective mask, and ensure that individual protective gear is nearby.
- **MOPP0.** Carry a protective mask, and ensure that individual protective gear is available.
- **MOPP1.** Don an overgarment.
- **MOPP2.** Don protective boots.

- **MOPP3.** Don a protective mask.
- **MOPP4.** Don protective gloves.

2-74. Leaders know that they cannot expect the same work rates in MOPP4 as they achieved in MOPP0. They reevaluate the ability to meet mission requirements and communicate changes to the force. MOPP reduction decisions are also among the most difficult to make because of the many considerations that affect the final decision. Commanders must evaluate the situation from the Soldier and mission perspectives. Factors include the criticality of the current mission, potential effects of personnel exposure, and the impact on the casualty care system. Commanders can then determine what follow-on COAs to employ.

2-75. Leaders determine the appropriate MOPP level by assessing METT-TC factors and weighing the impact of increased protection levels. Higher headquarters also provide MOPP level directives to subordinate elements.

2-76. The MOPP analysis process can be used as a tool to determine the appropriate protective posture, estimate unit/personnel effectiveness (mission degradation), estimate additional logistics requirements (water resupply, individual protective equipment replenishment), and assess/weigh the tradeoffs between agent exposures and degraded performance (wearing of MOPP4).

Note. For more information on MOPP levels, see FM 3-11.4.

SAFETY

2-77. Safety has a full spectrum mission. Operational conditions often impose significant hazards to Soldiers through the increased probability of an accidental event. In extreme OEs, these hazards raise the risk level as equipment and personnel are taxed. Leaders must know their Soldiers and trained crews, and operators must know the capabilities and limitations of their platforms and systems. To maintain a continuous operational tempo, commanders must know how to employ and sustain personnel and equipment. When planning operations, commanders—

- Consider human endurance limits and environmental conditions.
- Balance the possible benefits of sustained, high-tempo operations with the level of risk.
- Accept no unnecessary risks.
- Conduct high-risk operations only when the potential gain or benefit outweighs the potential loss.

2-78. Integrating safety into the operations process through the protection warfighting function and the CRM process provides an opportunity to identify and assess hazards to the force and develop risk reduction measures. (See FM 5-19 for more information.) The responsibility for safety starts with the commander and continues through the chain of command to individuals. Safety works best when all leaders and Soldiers receive training to recognize hazards and implement controls to reduce or mitigate risks in their daily operations. (See AR 385-10 for more information.)

2-79. Commanders at all levels normally have a safety officer assigned to their personal or special staff. The safety officer—

- Assists commanders in evaluating and maintaining awareness of safety-related issues, while facilitating safety integration.
- Maintains a close, day-to-day working relationship with the protection cell.
- Is a member of many forcing functions and forums, including the protection working group.
- Travels throughout the AO.
- Observes safety-related issues.
- Provides technical assistance to leaders and planners as they develop and execute safety programs, plans, orders, and SOPs.

OPERATIONS SECURITY

2-80. *OPSEC* is the process of identifying essential elements of friendly information and subsequently analyzing friendly actions attendant to military operations and other activities to: a. identify those actions that can be observed by adversary intelligence systems; b. determine indicators hostile intelligence systems might obtain that could be interpreted or pieced together to derive critical information in time to be useful to adversaries; and c. select and execute measures that eliminate or reduce to an acceptable level the vulnerabilities of friendly actions to adversary exploitation. (FM 3-13) (See AR 530-1 for more information.)

2-81. OPSEC applies to all operations across the spectrum of conflict. All units conduct OPSEC to preserve essential secrecy. Commanders establish routine OPSEC measures in unit SOPs. The OPSEC officer coordinates additional OPSEC measures with the G-2; assistant chief of staff, operations (G-3); and other staff and command elements. The OPSEC officer develops measures during the military decisionmaking process (MDMP). The G-2 assists the OPSEC process by comparing friendly OPSEC indicators with enemy intelligence collection capabilities. The chief of protection, OPSEC officer, and protection cell staff integrate OPSEC into all operations. (See appendix D for more information.)

EXPLOSIVE ORDNANCE DISPOSAL

2-82. The mission of EOD is to eliminate or reduce the effects of explosive ordnance (EO) hazards to protect combat power. EO hazards are ever-present dangers on the modern battlefield. They limit battlefield mobility, deny the use of critical assets, and threaten to injure or kill Soldiers at levels unprecedented in the past. This fact is graphically shown by the hundreds of casualties caused by the use of improvised explosive devices (IEDs) in Iraq and Afghanistan. Additionally, U.S. and coalition use of munitions that disperse submunitions across a wide area has led to increased amounts of unexploded ordnance (UXO) on the battlefield. EOD forces are trained, equipped, and organized to deal with the increased quantity, sophistication, and lethality of EO and support U.S. and coalition forces across the spectrum of conflict. (See FM 4-30.51 for more information.)

2-83. EOD units are specifically trained in the render-safe procedures (RSP)/disposal of EO/IEDs, including those containing CBRN materials. While other forces may have the ability to destroy UXO by detonation, they are not properly equipped, trained, or authorized to perform RSP or other disposal procedures. EOD elements normally—

- **Identify EO/IEDs/captured enemy ammunition and threats.**
  - Perform initial assessment of found munitions. Found munitions include single munitions discovered or captured during military operations (patrols, raids, maneuvers) or obtained through buyback or amnesty programs.
  - Assist commanders with AT, including intelligence support, electronic warfare defense plans, bomb threat/search procedures, facility site surveys, and development and implementation of EOD emergency response and AT plans.
- **Render-safe/dispose of EO/IEDs.** EOD is the only force equipped, manned, and trained to positively identify, render-safe, and dispose of U.S. and foreign EO/IEDs.
  - Assist commanders with the implementation of protective works and consequence management.
  - Provide technical advice and assistance to combat engineers during route clearance, area clearance, and minefield clearance operations.
  - Support responses to nuclear and chemical accidents/incidents, including technical advice and procedures to mitigate hazards associated with such items.
  - Provide EOD Soldiers in support of humanitarian efforts that involve EO.

Note. EOD provides technical assistance for the salvage, demolition, neutralization, or other disposition of government-owned shipments in transit.

- **Perform technical intelligence.** EOD units recover EO/IEDs/components for technical exploitation and prepare them for evacuation to a technical evaluation facility.
- **Perform postblast analysis.**
    - Assist commanders during explosive accident or incident investigations.
    - Gather technical intelligence on new/first-seen foreign ordnance and IEDs.
    - Conduct weapons intelligence and postblast analysis.
    - Advise and assist civilian authorities in conducting postblast investigations involving military ordnance and explosives.

Note. A priority of Army mortuary affairs is immediate recovery and clearance of deceased persons. The presence of UXO found on, embedded in, or in the vicinity of deceased persons adversely impacts the recovery of deceased U.S. or coalition personnel. Therefore, Army planners should involve EOD in the planning stages for the recovery and processing of deceased personnel.

This page intentionally left blank.

Chapter 3

Protection in Full Spectrum Operations

Adversaries seek to gain advantage through combat action and their ability to identify friendly vulnerabilities and infiltrate and penetrate the seams and gaps in friendly protection posture. As the violence and intensity of conflict increase, the ability to sufficiently protect the combat force and associated elements without hindering maneuver and stifling initiative becomes increasingly complex. The protection of the civilian population in some OEs could be the decisive operation that is linked to the protection of the military force. Detainees also require a level of protection. Commanders use the mission variables to develop protection strategies that integrate all forms of protection to deter, prevent, secure, defend, and restore the force during full spectrum operations. Commanders evaluate the significance of each mission, the vulnerabilities inherent in infrastructure and the environment, and their ability to protect the force.

FULL SPECTRUM OPERATIONS

3-1. *Full spectrum operations* is the Army's operational concept of combining offensive, defensive, and stability or civil support operations simultaneously as part of an interdependent joint force to seize, retain, and exploit the initiative, accepting prudent risk to create opportunity. They employ synchronized action—lethal and nonlethal—proportional to the mission and informed by a thorough understanding of all variables of the OE. Mission command that conveys intent and an appreciation of all aspects of the situation guides the adaptive use of Army forces. (FM 3-0) Ultimately, full spectrum operations create a safe and secure environment where the stabilization and restoration of peaceful processes can prevail and endure. (See figure 3-1.)

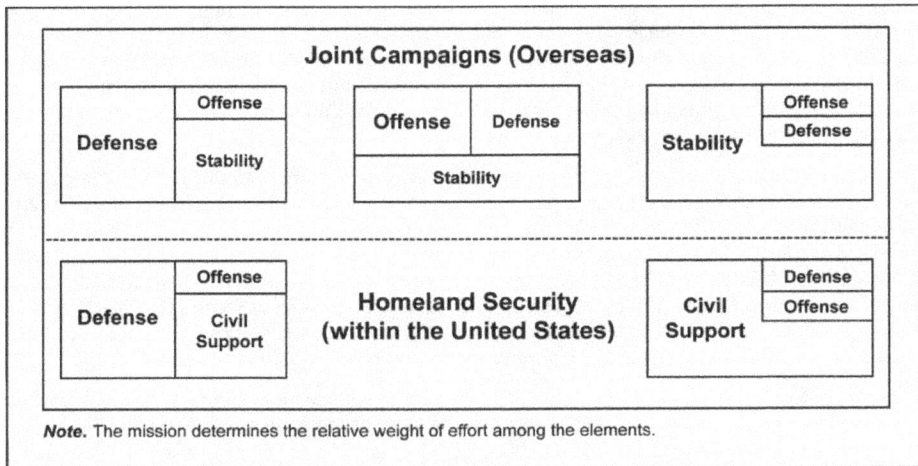

Figure 3-1. Full spectrum operations

3-2. Full spectrum operations require continuous, simultaneous combinations of offensive, defensive, and stability or civil support tasks:

- **Outside the continental United States (OCONUS).** Operations conducted OCONUS and in its territories simultaneously combine three elements—offense, defense, and stability. Commanders balance the right mix of constructive and destructive capabilities along with lethal and nonlethal actions to create dilemmas for opponents. Stability operations are characterized by nonlethal actions, but the ability to engage potential threats with lethal force remains a viable deterrent.
- **CONUS.** Operations in CONUS and in its territories require the element of civil support or a combination of offensive and defensive elements, depending on the nature of the mission. Civil support operations are characterized by nonlethal support actions. The use of offensive and defensive elements in CONUS is limited to very specific circumstances associated with homeland defense or self-defense by installations and personnel from hostile or life-threatening attacks. Offensive and defensive elements may only be used in accordance with U.S. law and DOD policy.

3-3. The Army can perform many tasks simultaneously, but not necessarily with equal emphasis or effectiveness. Commanders and leaders must be flexible and adaptive as they seek opportunities to seize, retain, and exploit the initiative. Leaders must have enhanced situational understanding in simultaneous full spectrum operations due to the diversity of threats, the proximity to civilians, and the impact of information during operations. The fluid, dynamic, and changing nature of operations may require the surge of certain capabilities, such as protection, to effectively link decisive operations to shaping or stabilizing activities in the AO. In other operations, the threat may be less discernible, unlikely to mass, and immune to the center of gravity analysis, which requires a constant and continuous protection effort or presence.

3-4. Full spectrum operations are also characterized by initiative, simultaneity, and synchronization. Operational and individual initiative involves intrinsic risk and opportunity, and significant opportunities do not typically last long. Full spectrum operations must be capable of simultaneity (enabled through the exercise of mission command) in order to act on opportunity. Mission command requires mutual trust and full knowledge of the operational concept and demands that subordinate leaders at all echelons exercise disciplined, aggressive, and independent initiative to accomplish the mission within the commander's intent.

3-5. Commanders must accept risk to exploit time-sensitive opportunities by acting before adversaries discover vulnerabilities, take evasive or defensive action, and implement countermeasures. Commanders and leaders can continue to act on operational and individual initiative if they make better risk decisions faster than the enemy, ultimately breaking the enemy's will and morale through relentless pressure. Commanders can leverage technological advancements or processes that improve endurance and protection capabilities to increase the probability of mission accomplishment. Advanced information technologies increase commanders' situational awareness, and the improved awareness enables commanders to make better risk decisions faster than the enemy.

3-6. Accurate assessment is essential for effective decisionmaking and the apportionment of combat power to protection tasks. Commanders fulfill protection requirements by applying or deriving reinforcing or complementing protection capabilities from forces in primary, supporting, or economy-of-force roles or from the OE itself. This is accomplished by identifying all protection capabilities available to the commander and then proportionately synchronizing them within the concept of operations and with all other full spectrum activities. Protection can be derived as a by-product or a complementary result of some combat operations (such as security operations), or it can be deliberately applied as commanders integrate and synchronize tasks and systems that comprise the protection warfighting function.

3-7. Full spectrum operations are normally translated into action through the development and arrangement of primary and subordinate tasks that ultimately become missions. (See table 3-1.)

Table 3-1. Elements of full spectrum operations

Operation	Primary Task	Purpose
Offensive	<ul><li>Movement to contact</li><li>Attack</li><li>Exploitation</li><li>Pursuit</li></ul>	<ul><li>Dislocate, isolate, disrupt, and destroy enemy forces.</li><li>Seize key terrain.</li><li>Deprive the enemy of resources.</li><li>Develop intelligence.</li><li>Deceive and divert the enemy.</li><li>Create a secure environment for stability operations.</li></ul>
Defensive	<ul><li>Mobile defense</li><li>Area defense</li><li>Retrograde</li></ul>	<ul><li>Deter or defeat enemy offensive operations.</li><li>Gain time.</li><li>Achieve economy of force.</li><li>Retain key terrain.</li><li>Protect the populace, critical assets, and infrastructure.</li><li>Develop intelligence.</li></ul>
Stability	<ul><li>Civil security</li><li>Civil control</li><li>Restoration of essential services</li><li>Support to governance</li><li>Support to economic and infrastructure development</li></ul>	<ul><li>Provide a secure environment.</li><li>Secure land areas.</li><li>Meet the critical needs of the populace.</li><li>Gain support for host nation government.</li><li>Shape the environment for interagency and host nation success.</li></ul>
Civil Support	<ul><li>Support in response to disasters or terrorist attacks</li><li>Support of civil law enforcement</li><li>Other support as required</li></ul>	<ul><li>Save lives.</li><li>Restore essential services.</li><li>Maintain or restore law and order.</li><li>Protect infrastructure and property.</li><li>Maintain or restore local government.</li><li>Shape the environment for interagency success.</li></ul>

OPERATIONAL DESIGN

3-8. Commanders and leaders use all aspects of military art and science to protect the force. At the operational level, leaders consider protection as they implement the elements of operations design to reinforce and complement protection. As they understand and visualize the OE, commanders develop broad concepts to effectively employ land power. Through the operational art, they define problems and challenges, formulate and refine designs, and link them through METT-TC variables to tangible and achievable objectives at the tactical level. Protection can often be derived from the effect or outcome of an operational approach that makes effective use of time, terrain, tides, or tempo. Ports, lodgment and staging areas, airfields, and drop zones are often decisive points that are selected or shaped for their ability to offer some level of protection to the force, mission, or center of gravity. Sanctuaries and safe havens are selected for their ability to provide protection, defense, or egress that is necessary to preserve the force or population. The elements of combat power can be sequenced in a reinforcing and complementary manner that provides protection for offensive action through preparatory activities, preemption, or diversion. Joint capabilities can also help set conditions that reduce risk and increase protection.

3-9. At the tactical level, AOs are often designated and assigned based on factors in the OE and unit capability. Unit boundaries, fire control restrictions, and graphic control measures help create zones of action, engagement areas, and kill zones for friendly forces that help commanders reduce the likelihood of fratricide or accidental damage. Rules of engagement (ROE), warning systems, and weapons control status protect the force and populations through the controlled application of lethal and nonlethal action. To this end, commanders are often given additional authority or C2, such as tactical control, to ensure the synchronization (necessary for rapid response, defense, and protection) of all elements operating in or near the AO.

SECURITY OPERATIONS

3-10. One of the most common methods of providing protection for ground combat forces during full spectrum operations is through security operations. The ultimate goal of security operations is to protect the force from surprise and reduce the unknown in any situation. Doctrine recognizes five forms of security operations in the military art:

- Screen.
- Guard.
- Cover.
- Area security.
- Local security.

3-11. Commanders use all five forms of security to protect the force during offensive operations; although, screen, guard, and cover are typically associated with combat formations specifically organized for combined arms maneuver. For this reason, screen, guard, and cover are also aligned with the movement and maneuver warfighting function while area security is aligned with the protection warfighting function for tactical task apportionment.

3-12. Screen, guard, and cover operations reflect increasing levels of combat power that can be applied to protect an asset or force from a directed threat and are typically conducted by combat units designed for combined arms maneuver. The primary purpose of a screen operation (see figure 3-2) is to provide early warning, thereby preventing surprise. Guard and cover operations (see figure 3-3) involve combined arms units in combat, fighting to gain time with differing levels of capability and autonomy for independent action.

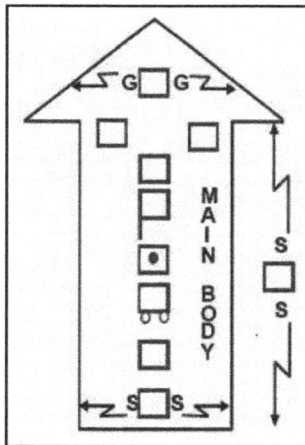

Figure 3-2. Screen security operation

3-13. Area security operations usually focus on the formation, asset, or location they are protecting and do not normally focus on the enemy force. Area security operations take advantage of the various local security measures being performed by all units in the AO. Local security measures are inherent to all operations and include active and passive measures taken against enemy actions. Local security allows commanders to provide immediate, responsive security to the force.

Note. See FM 3-90 for more information on security operations.

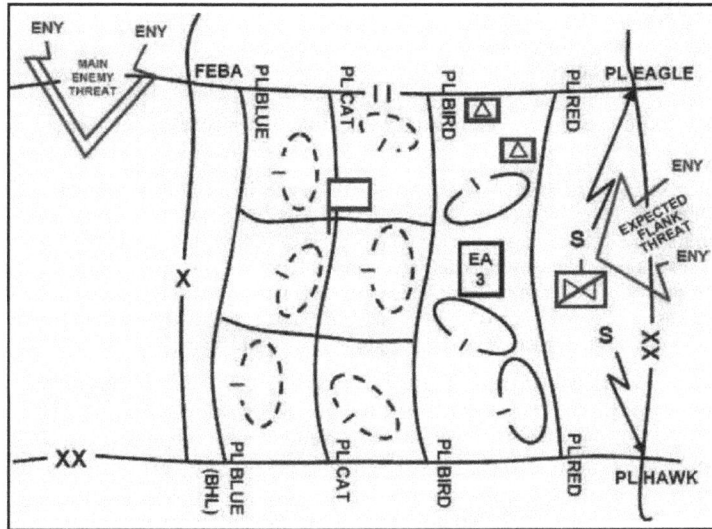

Figure 3-3. Guard security operation

OFFENSE

3-14. *Offensive operations* are combat operations conducted to defeat and destroy enemy forces and seize terrain, resources, and population centers. They impose the commander's will on the enemy. (FM 3-0) Surprise, concentration, tempo, and audacity characterize the offense. Movement and maneuver dominate during offensive operations. The application of protection capabilities to offensive operations is challenging because of the dynamic nature of offense action and the need for bold initiative that depends on the willingness to accept risk. Protection can be derived through audacity or surprise or by increasing the tempo of offensive operations. On the offense, leaders must balance the need for caution with the potential significance that opportunity offers and must weight their decision in favor of initiative and action. Army forces conduct offensive operations for several purposes, such as destroying or disrupting an enemy force, seizing key terrain, or creating a secure environment for stability operations. At the operational level, they defeat enemy forces that threaten important areas or governments. Primary offensive tasks include movement to contact, attack, exploitation, and pursuit. (See FM 3-0 for more information.)

3-15. Seizing, retaining, and exploiting initiative and opportunity are the essences of the offensive. Activities that do not directly contribute to that goal often become supporting, secondary, or nested efforts. In offensive operations, protection must be applied carefully and selectively to ensure that it does not have a debilitating effect on a commander's freedom of action. This is accomplished through protection integration and synchronization. Protection efforts are integrated with other combat power elements and synchronized simultaneously or sequentially where and when significant hazards and threats are projected in the offensive plan. This is typically a function of the protection cell and the G-3 at echelons above brigade, and it is achieved through a host of formal and informal processes at brigade and below. During offensive operations, typical points of vulnerability include flanks, critical C2 nodes and capabilities, lines of communications, sustainment areas, fratricidal events, unstable populations, and accidents. Protection integration is discussed in chapter 4.

PROTECTION DURING THE OFFENSE

3-16. Protection activities, tasks, and systems are applied and conducted to preserve combat power by reducing risk or mitigating vulnerability. Air and missile systems defend maneuver forces, critical infrastructure, and logistics bases. Although all commanders have some organic capability for air defense and warning, enhanced capabilities are often provided by higher-echelon commanders and air component organizations.

3-17. The preservation of combat power often requires the immediate restoration of critical skills and capabilities. All mission-capable personnel contribute to combat power in operations, but certain skills and capabilities can turn the tide of a battle or an engagement and their immediate recovery becomes essential. Therefore, PR operations are closely integrated into all phases, branches, and sequels associated with offensive operations to ensure that isolated and captured Soldiers are quickly recovered and returned to the fight. Combat arms crews and aviation crews and pilots are often a high-demand personnel asset during offensive operations, and their recovery may require specific guidance.

3-18. Combat conditions and operational stress can quickly take their toll on organizations and leaders engaged in prolonged offensive operations. Behavioral-health expertise provides preventative and restorative methods for identifying, treating, and restoring the effectiveness of personnel exposed to prolonged stress.

3-19. An enemy force may resort to the use of CBRNE capabilities or scorched-earth techniques to delay, divert, or culminate an offensive operation against them. Friendly CBRN reconnaissance assets must be positioned and synchronized to allow commanders an early CBRN detection and avoidance capability that enables rapid and decisive movement and maneuver and adjusts MOPP levels while preparing for decontamination. Force health practitioners monitor offensive running estimates for evidence of a deliberate or incidental epidemic, while ensuring that food and water sources are healthful.

3-20. Offensive operations often depend on shock, audacity, and surprise that are enabled through disciplined OPSEC and the physical security of weapons, devices, sensitive items, codes, passwords, and other sensitive or classified materials and information. Increased INFOCON during offensive operations enhances C2 and protection posture through prevention and situational awareness. Measures taken through CND to protect networks and computers from disruption and degradation can support and sustain the tempo of offensive operations and allow leaders greater situational awareness through the uninterrupted access to information. Information assurance helps authenticate the identity of information users and sustains the availability of access only by authorized users.

3-21. The tempo and speed of offensive operations can result in combat identification errors and fratricide. Deliberate precautions are taken to prevent surface-to-surface, surface-to-air, and air-to-surface friendly fire incidents through positive and procedural control mechanisms, standard unit marking schemes and patterns, and sound navigation and reporting procedures. Friendly and enemy forces often use obscurants for protection during movement and maneuver or to create surprise through diversion.

3-22. Through survivability, units shape the immediate environment and location to provide or create self-protection. On the offense, selected sites and positions from which combat power must be generated and sustained may need to be hardened or protected for the duration of offensive operations. Tactical operations centers (TOCs), radars, and some logistical elements are hardened or frequently moved to keep pace with operations and to ensure their survivability. In support areas, commanders conduct area damage control to prevent and respond to the negative effects of enemy action that can diminish combat power.

3-23. Area security operations allow commanders to provide protection to critical assets without a significant diversion of combat power. During offensive operations, various military organizations may be involved in conducting area security operations in an economy of force role to protect lines of communications, convoys, or critical fixed sites and radars. Bases and base clusters employ local security measures (including EOD, assessments and recommendations, random AT measures, and increased FPCON), but may be vulnerable to enemy remnant forces requiring a response that is beyond base. Area security operations support offensive operations by providing a response capability to base clusters and sustainment areas and to designated geographical areas such as routes, bridge sites, or lodgments.

3-24. The following vignette shows how a commander carefully balances threat and vulnerability to decide on acceptable risk and complete the mission according to the higher commander's intent.

Thunder Runs in Baghdad

On 6 April 2003, the 3d Infantry Division was on the outskirts of Baghdad. Major General Buford Blount, 3d Infantry Division (Mechanized) commander, ordered Colonel David Perkins, 2d Brigade commander, to execute a limited-objective attack into Baghdad.

The brigade was located in Objective Saints. Task Force 1-64 Armor was to lead from Objective Saints and seize Objective Diane. Task Force 4-64 Armor would follow and seize two palaces designated Objectives Woody West and Woody East. Task Force 3-15 Infantry would secure Objective Saints and the lines of communications between Objectives Saints and Diane. Three key highway interchanges along the lines of communications were designated as Moe, Larry, and Curly.

The initiative, speed, shock, and surprise of the drive to Baghdad, coupled with the "thunder runs" inside the city, caught the Iraqi forces and leaders by surprise. The price for this tactical gamble was extremely vulnerable supply lines and combat trains.

To prepare for this dangerous mission, each task force utilized a scout platoon as an escort force for a limited logistics package (four fuel and two ammunition trucks). The logistics package was kept in Objective Saints on a "be prepared" status to move north into the city if necessary. In addition, units stripped all unnecessary equipment from the tanks and Bradleys. This reduced the fire potential since baggage in the bustle racks would easily catch fire if hit by rocket-propelled grenades, recoilless rifles, or other incendiaries. Each vehicle had more than its basic load of small arms and about a 5-day supply of water.

To eliminate concerns about lighter-skinned vehicles and to increase mobility and survivability, Task Force 1-64 took only limited vehicles. These included tanks, Bradleys, and one or two M113s per company (first sergeant/maintenance). The engineer companies remained at Objective Saints and, along with the mortar platoons, served as a quick reaction force to assist with a withdrawal from the Baghdad objectives, if needed, or to immediately reinforce success.

The battalions rigged tow cables on all vehicles for the hasty towing of disabled vehicles. This and all other battle drills were thoroughly rehearsed. The commander accepted the risk that no vehicles would be repaired until the unit maintenance collection point could be brought forward. The units briefed and rehearsed a Baghdad evacuation plan that had units maneuvering back to Objective Saints. Alternate routes to and from the objectives were identified. Colonel Perkins also established decision points to prevent the loss of combat power. For example, if they could not get resupplied in 24 hours, the plan was to pull back out of the city. Due to flight restrictions, casualty evacuation was only possible by ground transportation and the first sergeants' vehicles were tasked with this mission. They planned to use two combat vehicles to escort the first sergeants' vehicles out of the city to Objective Saints and hand them off to the logistics staff officer (S-4).

This example shows a commander taking a calculated risk despite vulnerable supply lines. To mitigate the risk, the unit applied principles of protection. In the end, the unit achieved not only a tactical objective, but also a strategic objective—the downfall of the regime in Baghdad. Perkins applied the art of war to achieve the tactical and operational advantage, while preserving his force through risk mitigation. His actions illustrated the weakness of the Iraqi government and military to the world. The quick fall of the regime caused by the response to this decisive maneuver operation resulted in the rapid culmination of Iraqi ground forces.

DEFENSE

3-25. *Defensive operations* are combat operations conducted to defeat an enemy attack, gain time, economize forces, and develop conditions favorable for offensive or stability operations. (FM 3-0) Successful defensive operations are often characterized by preparation, security, disruption, massed effects, and flexibility. Commanders may also choose to defend for other purposes, to include retaining key terrain or protecting the populace, critical assets, and infrastructure. There are three tasks associated with the defense—area defense, mobile defense, and retrograde movement. While area and mobile defense basically describe typical defensive patterns involving combat, retrograde movement generally involves an organized movement away from the enemy to preserve the force.

3-26. In a mobile defense, the defender withholds a large portion of available forces for use as a striking force in a counterattack. Mobile defenses require enough depth to let enemy forces advance into a position that exposes them to counterattack. The defense separates attacking forces from their support and disrupts the enemy's C2. As enemy forces extend themselves in the defended area and lose momentum and organization, the defender surprises and overwhelms them with a powerful counterattack.

3-27. A mobile defense normally integrates elements of offense, defense, and delay while focusing combined arms maneuver on the destruction of enemy forces. Most of the force forms a striking force, while the rest of the force defends in depth and exposes the enemy to counterattack. An area defense concentrates on denying enemy access to a particular area of terrain, restricting their freedom of maneuver, and drawing them into kill zones and engagement areas where they can be defeated in detail from mutually supporting positions.

Note. See FM 3-0 for more information on defensive operations.

3-28. Operational commanders often employ a covering force to protect the main body during a withdrawal or retrograde or on the defensive by disrupting enemy attacks, destroying initiatives, and setting the conditions for decisive operations. (See FM 3-90 for more information.) Enemy forces must risk the loss of momentum and culmination as they fight through the covering force, often committing their reserves in the process. Covering force operations are resource-intensive because of their requirement for independent action and may be represented at the tactical level as guard operations in the defense (see figure 3-4).

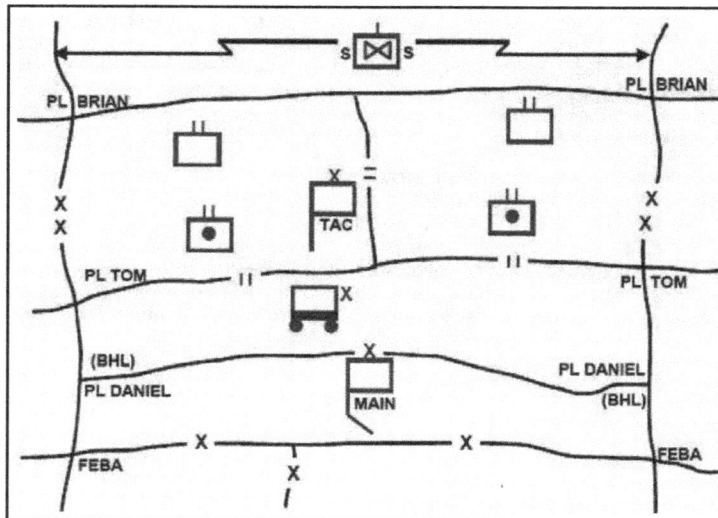

Figure 3-4. Cover security operation

PROTECTION DURING THE DEFENSE

3-29. No matter which defensive task is performed, the survivability of C2 centers and key communications nodes in defensive operations is critical to their success. Survivability and AT tasks and plans are essential during the defense and may require a deliberate and detailed approach to ensure that combat power is apportioned where it is most needed. Commanders may use decision support tools and analysis to assess critical assets and key vulnerabilities. In mature theaters or FOBs, commanders plan and prepare for enemy attacks by predicting where the next attack will occur and apply measures to mitigate the effectiveness of the attack. These attacks may be from conventional, irregular, or terrorist forces and drive changes in local FPCON or individual protective measures. Incident management plans and area damage control in execution are key components to a successful protection plan. These plans cover all threat capabilities and environmental considerations and integrate protection tasks and systems. EOD assets and personnel support AT efforts on bases and in base clusters and dispose of UXO during defensive operations.

3-30. In defensive operations, commanders protect forces and critical assets by conducting area security operations because of their flexibility. Forces conducting area security in the defense can deter, detect, or defeat enemy reconnaissance while creating standoff distances from enemy direct- and indirect-fire systems. Area security operations can be used to protect the rapid movement of combat trains or protect cached commodities until needed.

3-31. Mobile defensive schemes are characterized by a high degree of movement and maneuver; therefore, they seek fratricide avoidance in a manner similar to offensive operations through solid land navigation and position reporting, combat identification, and positive control. Area defense protects the force from fratricide by the deliberate structure of the defensive pattern that emphasizes preparation, identifiable engagement areas and kill zones, engagement criteria, and mutually supporting positions. The commitment of the reserve force during an area defense operation may create the conditions for a fratricide event and are, therefore, typically well rehearsed.

3-32. Any defensive operation could potentially begin with enemy bombardment, resulting in a siege that can have dramatic results on the mental and behavioral health of unit personnel. Soldiers can become combat ineffective from the close proximity of heavy indirect fire even if exposure is for short durations. Systems for combat stress identification and treatment are deliberately emplaced to reduce the return-to-duty time of affected personnel.

3-33. Commanders deploy air defense and alert warning systems to prevent and warn of an air intrusion, air insertion, or air and missile attack. Air defense coverage may be positioned along likely air avenues of approach and near designated critical assets.

3-34. Units develop, train, and rehearse a CBRN defense plan to protect personnel and equipment from an attack or incident involving CBRN hazards. MOPP analysis results in initial MOPP and personal protective equipment levels, and decontaminants are positioned accordingly. Force health personnel maintain situational awareness and surveillance of personnel strength information for indications of force contamination, epidemic, or other anomalies apparent in force health trend data.

3-35. Area defensive patterns require the placement of obstacles and the deliberate development and preparation of fighting and support by fire positions, engagement areas, and kill boxes. Engineer assets emplace obstacles and harden defensive positions throughout the defensive schemes. They also assure the mobility of striking forces that support mobile defenses and reserve forces that support area defensive plans.

3-36. Effective and disciplined OPSEC protects essential elements of friendly information (EEFI), preventing enemy reconnaissance and other information collection capabilities from gaining an advantage through identifiable or observable pieces of friendly information or activities. This is key during defensive and retrograde operations to prevent surprise. OPSEC and information protection activities deny the enemy access to information systems and prevent network intrusion, degradation, or destruction through computer network defensive TTP, while electronic protection capabilities prevent an attacking enemy from using the electromagnetic spectrum to degrade or neutralize friendly combat capabilities.

3-37. Preventable accidents can thwart mission success during combat operations. Leaders must continue to assess the environment and routine activities for the evidence of hazards that can lead to the preventable loss of combat power through accidents and events. Personnel rest and recovery plans, leader experience, and skill levels are safety considerations that influence risk management decisions during combat operations.

STABILITY

3-38. *Stability operations* is an overarching term encompassing various military missions, tasks, and activities conducted outside the United States in coordination with other instruments of national power to maintain or reestablish a safe and secure environment and provide essential governmental services, emergency infrastructure reconstruction, and humanitarian relief. (JP 3-0) Stability operations aim to stabilize the environment enough that the host nation can begin to resolve the root causes of conflict and failure of the state. When a host nation or other agency cannot provide the basic functions of government, military forces may be introduced to establish or restore basic civil functions and protect them until the host nation or a civil authority is capable of providing these services for the local populace. Stability operations are often more important to the lasting success of military operations than traditional combat operations because they enable the introduction of other instruments of national power to an OE, creating a stable foundation for the transfer of activities to civilian or host nation control.

3-39. Stability operations are conducted within the context of full spectrum operations (see figure 3-1, page 3-1). Offensive operations continue, but are generally characterized as episodic activities against specific or focused targets, individuals, or groups. Offensive operations may include limited major operations against former warring parties or raids and deliberate cordon-and-search operations throughout the OE. Defensive operations may be conducted to protect facilities, enclaves, sanctuaries, or groups or to gain time for response forces to take decisive action.

3-40. Military forces must quickly seize and retain the initiative in stability operations to gain control of civil mechanisms of power and the environment and to prevent local conditions from destabilizing or deteriorating. Acting boldly can prevent organized resistance from developing, while creating opportunities for actions necessary to reduce suffering, strengthen institutions, and begin the transition to civil authority. Bold initiatives during stability operations involve risk. The close proximity to civilians with immediate access to global information conduits can magnify the consequences of inaction, accidents, collateral damage, and casualties. Leaders must carefully balance lethal and nonlethal actions during stability operations. Overcautious prevention activities or procedures limit the freedom of action just as unrestrained action can result in provocation tactics by adversaries.

3-41. Fragile states suffer from institutional weaknesses that threaten the survival of their central government. (See FM 3-07 for more information.) Stability operation strategies are developed to achieve conflict resolution by enhancing host nation legitimacy, civil institution development through capacity-building activities, and progress toward justice and the rule of law. They support and reflect overarching national security, defense, and military strategies and policies eventually articulated within the framework of the campaign plan at the operational level. At this level, stability operation strategies often require the integration of operational and tactical tasks along the lines of effort that lead to the following end state conditions:

- Safe and secure environment.
- Established rule of law.
- Social well-being.
- Stable government.
- Sustainable economy.

3-42. Protection of the force during stability operations is essential for success at all levels of operations, from tactical to strategic. Like offensive and defensive operations, stability operations can derive some protection from the concept of operations alone, but the most sustainable protection success for the force is achieved by integrating the protection tasks and systems that comprise the protection warfighting function. Loss, damage, injuries, and casualties can influence the will of participating populations to sustain operations. The enduring nature of stability operations may require a protection strategy that is more resource-intensive and prescribed than typical security operations.

3-43. Stability operations require commanders to balance protection needs between military forces and civil populations. Because U.S. forces and the local population frequently interact, planning for their protection is important and difficult. Enemies attack to weaken U.S. resolve and promote their individual agendas. Such enemies, who may be nearly indistinguishable from noncombatants, view U.S. forces and facilities as prime targets. An additional planning consideration during stability operations is to protect the force while using the minimum force consistent with the approved ROE. The escalation of force TTP must also be rehearsed and flexible enough to change with the local threat conditions. Collateral damage caused by military operations can negatively impact the mission and support enemy provocation tactics. Conversely, overly restrictive ROE can limit the commander's freedom of action and ability to protect the force.

3-44. Stability operations and irregular warfare often involve conflict between nonstate actors who possess limited conventional forces. For this reason, some Army functional capabilities are often retasked from their primary function to conduct or reinforce protection efforts such as fratricide avoidance, operational security, and AT based on METT-TC.

3-45. Adversaries often blend in with the local populace during stability operations and are difficult to identify, making heightened levels of awareness the norm. Civil areas typically contain structured and prepared routes, roadways, and avenues that can canalize traffic. Control measures (such as establishing traffic patterns) could alleviate traffic concerns, but may also expose vulnerabilities that enemies and adversaries will exploit. This can lead to predictable friendly movement patterns that can easily be templated by the enemy. Commanders may gradually apply protection to protect movement, or they may establish a movement corridor. (See figure 3-5.)

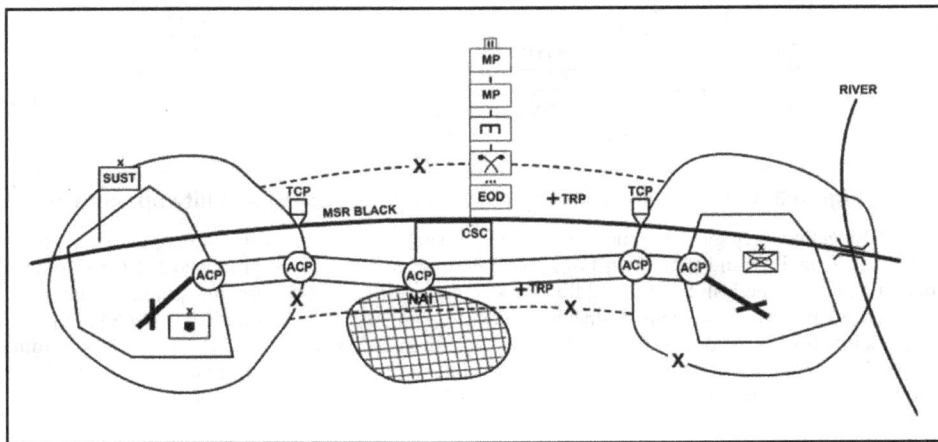

Figure 3-5. Movement corridor operation

3-46. Information engagement is an essential activity during stability operations and is a key protection enabler. Commanders and Soldiers engage the local population to inform friendly audiences and influence neutral audiences, enemies, and adversaries. This can include measures such as improving local information programs, improving populace and infrastructure security, defeating IED bomb-making and expertise-funding efforts, and defeating insurgent or terrorist recruitment efforts. Civil affairs (CA) organizations help develop formal and informal relationships. Leaders and Soldiers conduct information engagement tasks to facilitate the delivery of friendly messages and themes (matched by actions on the ground) to key leaders and population groups.

3-47. The close proximity of civilians and Soldiers can also promote FHP issues (such as communicable disease) through close contact with local civilians, detainees, or local foods. Stability operations are often enduring missions that can lead to complacency among Soldiers and result in an increase in accidents. Disciplined risk reduction efforts require effective leadership and should be continually monitored and assessed from the beginning to the end of an operation or deployment.

3-48. The protection of civil institutions, processes, and systems required to reach the end state conditions of the stability operations strategy can often be the most decisive factor in stability operations because its accomplishment is essential for long-term success. For that reason, stability operations require a "whole government" approach that sets the conditions necessary to enable the elements of national power (diplomatic, information, military, and economic). Stability operation tasks include—

- Establishing civil security.
- Establishing civil control.
- Restoring essential services.
- Supporting governance.
- Supporting economic and infrastructure development.

3-49. Information engagement is also essential to the success of these operations. Unified action and interagency participation is achieved by nesting the five stability tasks with the five stability sectors identified by the Department of State (DOS) Coordinator for Reconstruction and Stabilization. (See figure 3-6.)

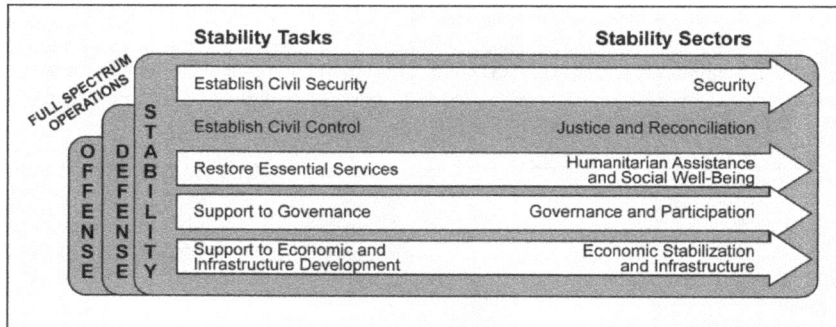

Figure 3-6. Whole-government, integrated approach to stability operations

3-50. Protection strategies for supporting stability operations are designed to link operational goals and end states with stability and protection tasks integrated through combined arms and the CRM process at the operational and tactical levels. Stability tasks and security sectors are integrated within the stability operations framework to help define and measure progress and to provide a context for conducting operations. (See figure 3-7.) The stability operations framework defines the environment according to two quantifiable, complementary scales—decreasing violence and increasing normalization of the state which is the fundamental measure of success in conflict transformation. (See FM 3-07 for more information.)

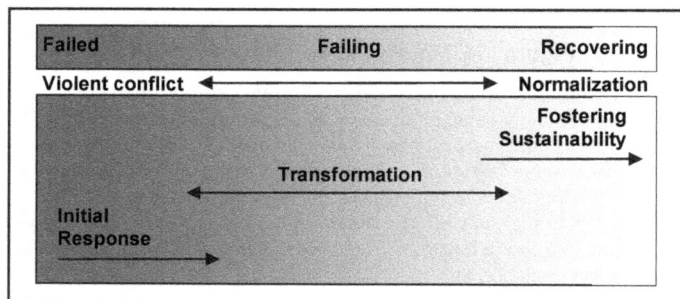

Figure 3-7. Stability operations framework

3-51. Protection strategies for stability operations often begin by determining where the current situation is best described along the fragile-state spectrum or continuum and then applying protection capabilities to the most significant military and civilian vulnerabilities. Primary stability operation tasks reflect a host of subtasks within the continuum of operations and throughout the five stability sectors. Protection measures are applied during vulnerability assessments focused on the primary stability operation tasks.

ESTABLISH CIVIL SECURITY

3-52. An initial response to a stability operation conducted in a failing state may emphasize the establishment of civil security as a means of protecting critical assets, facilities, personnel, or freedom of movement. Border or boundary control operations protect the integrity and sovereignty of the host nation while providing protection against illegal entrants, contraband, disease, and the enemy. Border operations can be conducted as a type of area defensive operation or through area security tasks and TTP integrating checkpoints, mobile patrols, and designated fixed sites.

3-53. Stability operations are often characterized by the absence of large-scale military operations that emphasize combined arms maneuver. However, tactical and nontactical movement occurs throughout the OE as a matter of military necessity and as a component of a normalized society. Controlling and maintaining the freedom of movement in the OE is essential for efficiency and for protecting friendly military forces and the population. This can include various methods (including curfews, routine restrictions, and travel authorizations) that are enforced and monitored throughout checkpoints or technologies. (See figure 3-8.) This may be accomplished through movement and maneuver enhancement, area security operations, or in conjunction with law and order operations as a function of traffic regulation enforcement. A deliberate information engagement program is often essential when implementing movement or traffic controls and restrictions on a given population in an AO. Commanders can leverage host nation security, police, and civic organizations through information engagement to assist with the implementation of movement controls and traffic enforcement for the safety and security of the force and the local population. Response force operations supporting troops engaged in controlling or limiting movement take deliberate precautions to prevent fratricide.

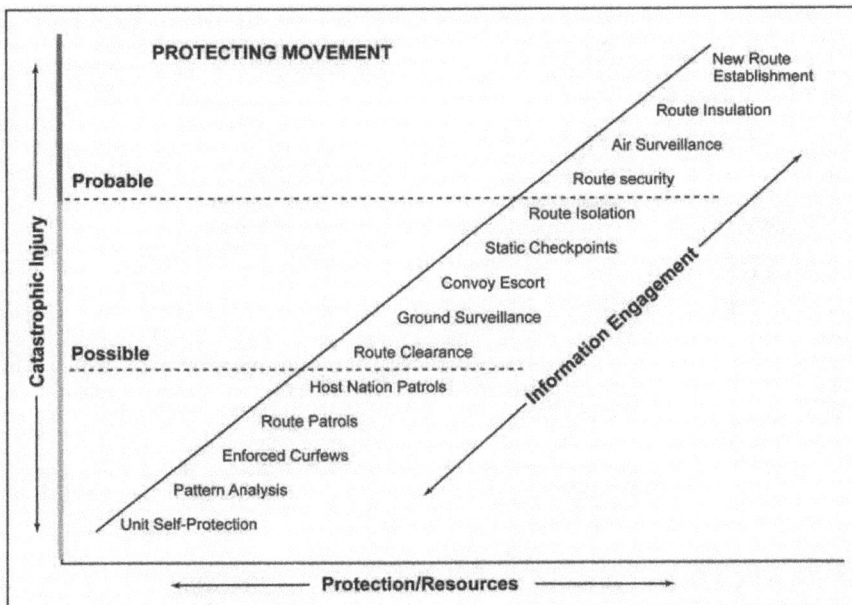

Figure 3-8. Controlling freedom of movement for protection

3-54. The protection of key personnel and facilities may be an essential task anywhere in the stability operations fragile-state spectrum or stability operations framework where there is a directed threat. Key civil leaders may require protective services, sound AT and OPSEC procedures that are included in PR plans and battle drills, and police and physical security reinforcement. Facilities that have national, cultural, religious, or military significance may need dedicated security to reduce civil tension. Police stations, armories, and hospitals may require immediate protection during heightened awareness. Records and documentation for verifying identity and authority, deviant behavior, key governmental actions, and other important historical events and information may need to be protected from destruction and misuse. Explosives, mines, UXO, or CBRN hazards may exist in the OE at the cessation of hostilities or may be introduced deliberately or accidentally. These threats and hazards may require an integrated EOD, demining, or foreign consequence management response.

ESTABLISH CIVIL CONTROL

3-55. Transformation occurs in the stability operations framework as civil security is achieved and certain risks are reduced, making other stability operation tasks possible. Civil control regulates behavior in an AO and builds the foundation for order, justice, and the rule of law. There is a host of enforcement mechanisms in a given society to maintain normalcy and civil behavior, including law enforcement officials, local political and civic leaders, educators, clergy, and others who reflect and maintain local law, customs, norms, and values. Most civil societies follow some form of predictable social activity cycle that often includes seasonal, ethnic, religious, or cultural events such as holidays, school or academic periods, or days of specific observance. The chief of protection examines the significance of each event for potential hazards, risks, and opportunities and applies the requisite protection capability. For example, religious holidays or pilgrimages may increase the number of third-country nationals entering the host nation while a patriotic event could lead to the massing of civilians at key governmental locations. The end of the academic school period may increase the number of adolescents in the streets of certain regions.

3-56. Military forces may be initially engaged in conducting policing and penal operations to prevent criminal activity or to reduce crime-conducive conditions in a particular area. These activities protect communities from criminal predators who can have a chilling effect on populations and destabilize specific areas. In these operations, military forces must be proficient in the escalation of force before resorting to lethal action within the ROE. Nonlethal TTP and technologies provide commanders with the ability to demonstrate a measured force response which can contribute to the protection of the force and the civil populace. The presence of well-trained, equipped, and disciplined troops with lethal or violent capability can often be sufficient to deter violence, confrontation, or conflict during a stability operation. Law enforcement activities transition from military personnel to civilian police who are supplied by the host nation or as part of a third-country or international policing effort. Police training, development, and mentoring may continue until normalization is achieved. Commanders may authorize, develop, and train civilian volunteers to augment civil control efforts or to serve as a police auxiliary.

RESTORE ESSENTIAL SERVICES

3-57. Areas that have been neglected or damaged as a result of conflict may require the protection of essential infrastructure. Power generation, water treatment, medical, and transportation facilities and systems may require protection from pilferage, sabotage, or neglect which may be accomplished through physical security, survivability, or area security TTP. Broadcast news, journalists, media outlets, and other information venues often adhere to a predictable media or news cycle. The chief of protection works with public affairs personnel to restore local media outlets and to anticipate the impact of negative or sensational broadcast media or other information releases to the force or in the OE. Information engagement also involves significant leader and Soldier engagement with the local population as a means for informing the public while also gathering information on the environment.

3-58. By integrating military and host nation police forces early, commanders get police or street level information on local criminal elements, including organized crime. Through combined police operations, commanders help establish a safe and secure environment for U.S. forces, host nation forces, and civilians. Such multinational operations also improve the perception of host nation government legitimacy. When no insurgent or terrorist threat exists, integrating protection actions may be limited to safety and FHP activities.

SUPPORT GOVERNANCE

3-59. When conditions in a failed or failing state become extreme and prevent the host nation government from conducting civic functions, military forces must be capable of providing support to governance and civic functions while acting as a transitional military authority according to the international law or mandate. (See FM 3-07 for more information.) In this capacity, military forces may be required to protect the integrity of specific governmental processes. Elections normally follow a predictable cycle of activity that can be examined for the evidence of corruption, election fraud, organized criminal involvement, or threat interference. Election events, voting sites, and ballots require protection and safe access to ensure the legitimacy of election results. International election monitors or support personnel may also require some level of personnel protection.

SUPPORT ECONOMIC AND INFRASTRUCTURE DEVELOPMENT

3-60. Protection capabilities are often applied to support economic and infrastructure developmental efforts during stability operations to foster sustainability. Building capacity within the economic sector often requires the protection of specific activities and conditions for local economies to thrive and develop. Business and economic activities typically follow a semipredictable cycle that may be seasonal, coinciding with events such as agricultural harvests or conditions that make commodity gathering or production optimal. These predictable events often telegraph other corresponding or supporting activities that may require protection from interference. Commodity markets can be influenced and manipulated, or commodity producers may be denied access to markets. Manufacturing facilities may be susceptible to illicit labor practices. Black markets can create shortages, while human trafficking may thrive due to underdeveloped economic conditions. Banks and other monetary institutions may require deliberate fixed-site or area security during periods of unrest and shortage.

CIVIL SUPPORT

3-61. DOD *civil support operations* are divided into the three broad categories of domestic emergencies, support of designated law enforcement agencies, and other support activities (JP 3-28). This includes responds during disasters and declared emergencies, support or restoration of public health and services and civil order, support during national special security events, and periodic planned support of other activities. Army forces conduct civil support operations exclusive of the elements of offense and defense. (See FM 3-0 for more information.)

3-62. When support for domestic emergencies is provided under the auspices of the national response framework, it is called *defense support of civil authorities (DSCA)*. The national response framework is the Department of Homeland Security guide to how the nation conducts an all-hazards response. It is built upon scalable, flexible, and adaptable coordinating structures to align key roles and responsibilities across the nation. Federal, state, tribal, and local governments; nongovernmental organizations; and the private sector use the National Incident Management System to execute response to incidents. The National Incident Management System provides a consistent nationwide template that allows public and private sectors to work together to prevent, protect against, respond to, recover from, and mitigate the effects of incidents, regardless of their cause, size, location, or complexity. Unless otherwise directed by the President, the U.S. military conducts DSCA operations in support of other federal agencies that are coordinating the federal response. The Federal Emergency Management Agency (FEMA) is typically the primary federal agency for requesting and coordinating DOD support.

3-63. The commitment of DOD resources for DSCA operations requires approval by the Secretary of Defense or direction from the President. In most instances, DOD provides DSCA in response to a request for assistance from another federal agency when local, tribal, state, and federal resources are fully committed or when a DOD-unique capability is required. All requests for assistances are evaluated by DOD to determine whether they meet the criteria for supportability (legality, lethality, risk, cost, appropriateness, and impact on readiness). Once the request for assistance is approved, DOD issues a mission assignment that specifies exactly what type and how much support is authorized. In some imminently serious situations, local commanders may unilaterally initiate an immediate response to save lives, prevent human suffering, or mitigate great property damage. However, Secretary of Defense approval

overall operation. (See figure 4-2.) This is often accomplished through the use of cross-functional teams, working groups, and boards.

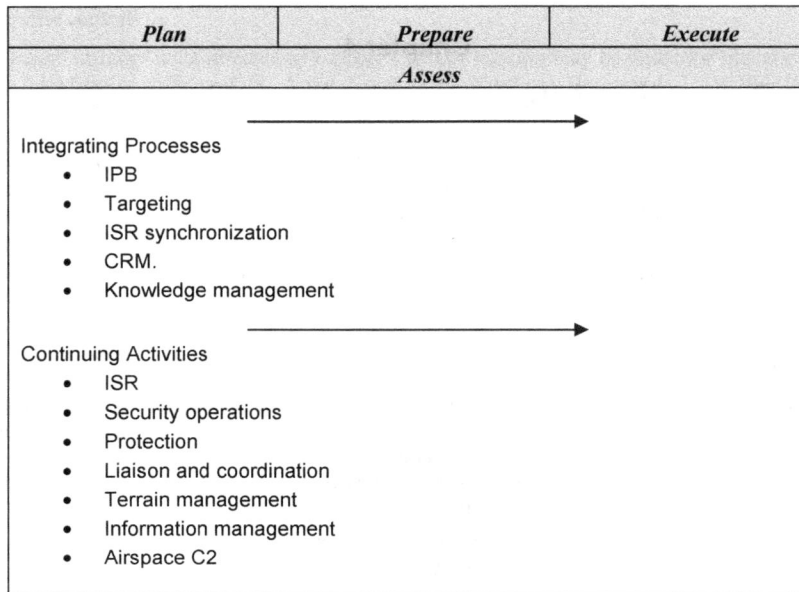

Plan	Prepare	Execute
Assess		

Integrating Processes
- IPB
- Targeting
- ISR synchronization
- CRM.
- Knowledge management

Continuing Activities
- ISR
- Security operations
- Protection
- Liaison and coordination
- Terrain management
- Information management
- Airspace C2

Figure 4-2. Continuing activities and integrating processes

BATTLE COMMAND AND PROTECTION STRATEGIES

4-4.   Commanders drive the operations process through the application of *battle command*, which is the art and science of understanding, visualizing, describing, directing, leading, and assessing forces to impose the commander's will on a hostile, thinking, and adaptive enemy. Battle command applies leadership to translate decisions into actions—by synchronizing forces and warfighting functions in time, space, and purpose—to accomplish missions. (FM 3-0) (See figure 4-3.) Commanders combine the military art and science to translate information and experience into superior decisions faster than the enemy. They also determine priorities, provide guidance, establish time horizons, create command climates, and accept risk in ways that are clear and help focus the staff and subordinate organizations. The commander's inherent responsibility to protect and preserve the force, while seeking every opportunity to act decisively, makes it imperative to consider protection in the operations process.

SUPPORT GOVERNANCE

3-59. When conditions in a failed or failing state become extreme and prevent the host nation government from conducting civic functions, military forces must be capable of providing support to governance and civic functions while acting as a transitional military authority according to the international law or mandate. (See FM 3-07 for more information.) In this capacity, military forces may be required to protect the integrity of specific governmental processes. Elections normally follow a predictable cycle of activity that can be examined for the evidence of corruption, election fraud, organized criminal involvement, or threat interference. Election events, voting sites, and ballots require protection and safe access to ensure the legitimacy of election results. International election monitors or support personnel may also require some level of personnel protection.

SUPPORT ECONOMIC AND INFRASTRUCTURE DEVELOPMENT

3-60. Protection capabilities are often applied to support economic and infrastructure developmental efforts during stability operations to foster sustainability. Building capacity within the economic sector often requires the protection of specific activities and conditions for local economies to thrive and develop. Business and economic activities typically follow a semipredictable cycle that may be seasonal, coinciding with events such as agricultural harvests or conditions that make commodity gathering or production optimal. These predictable events often telegraph other corresponding or supporting activities that may require protection from interference. Commodity markets can be influenced and manipulated, or commodity producers may be denied access to markets. Manufacturing facilities may be susceptible to illicit labor practices. Black markets can create shortages, while human trafficking may thrive due to underdeveloped economic conditions. Banks and other monetary institutions may require deliberate fixed-site or area security during periods of unrest and shortage.

CIVIL SUPPORT

3-61. DOD *civil support operations* are divided into the three broad categories of domestic emergencies, support of designated law enforcement agencies, and other support activities (JP 3-28). This includes responds during disasters and declared emergencies, support or restoration of public health and services and civil order, support during national special security events, and periodic planned support of other activities. Army forces conduct civil support operations exclusive of the elements of offense and defense. (See FM 3-0 for more information.)

3-62. When support for domestic emergencies is provided under the auspices of the national response framework, it is called *defense support of civil authorities (DSCA)*. The national response framework is the Department of Homeland Security guide to how the nation conducts an all-hazards response. It is built upon scalable, flexible, and adaptable coordinating structures to align key roles and responsibilities across the nation. Federal, state, tribal, and local governments; nongovernmental organizations; and the private sector use the National Incident Management System to execute response to incidents. The National Incident Management System provides a consistent nationwide template that allows public and private sectors to work together to prevent, protect against, respond to, recover from, and mitigate the effects of incidents, regardless of their cause, size, location, or complexity. Unless otherwise directed by the President, the U.S. military conducts DSCA operations in support of other federal agencies that are coordinating the federal response. The Federal Emergency Management Agency (FEMA) is typically the primary federal agency for requesting and coordinating DOD support.

3-63. The commitment of DOD resources for DSCA operations requires approval by the Secretary of Defense or direction from the President. In most instances, DOD provides DSCA in response to a request for assistance from another federal agency when local, tribal, state, and federal resources are fully committed or when a DOD-unique capability is required. All requests for assistances are evaluated by DOD to determine whether they meet the criteria for supportability (legality, lethality, risk, cost, appropriateness, and impact on readiness). Once the request for assistance is approved, DOD issues a mission assignment that specifies exactly what type and how much support is authorized. In some imminently serious situations, local commanders may unilaterally initiate an immediate response to save lives, prevent human suffering, or mitigate great property damage. However, Secretary of Defense approval or Presidential directive is still required for the commitment of potentially lethal capabilities or direct law enforcement support, including interdicting vehicles; conducting searches and seizures; making arrests or apprehensions; and performing surveillance, investigation or undercover work, security patrols, and crowd/traffic control.

3-64. Federal military units directed to support a DSCA mission may be under the operational control of a defense coordinating officer, U.S. Army North, U.S. Northern Command (USNORTHCOM), or U.S. Pacific Command depending on the situation. Requested support can include such capabilities as medical, aviation, communications, damage assessment, transportation, logistics, debris clearing, aerial firefighting, and CBRN consequence management response. According to the Posse Comitatus Act, members of the U.S. Army, Navy, Air Force, and Marine Corps (including state national guard forces called into federal service) are prohibited from exercising nominally state law enforcement, police, or peace officer powers that maintain law and order on nonfederal property (states and their counties and municipal divisions) within the United States. There are some exceptions in which the Posse Comitatus Act does not apply; these include national guard units under state authority and Title 10 troops under the order of the President of the United States pursuant to the Insurrection Act.

3-65. The commitment of DOD resources for other civil support operations (such as support to designated law enforcement agencies, support during national special security events, and periodic planned support of other activities) requires approval according to national laws and DOD policies.

3-66. FHP capabilities may support the preservation of life within the framework of the National Disaster Medical System (NDMS). The NDMS combines federal and nonfederal medical resources into a unified medical response system for incidents involving public health and medical emergencies. Under the auspices of the Department of Health and Human Services, the NDMS facilitates the deployment of various medical response teams to an event area. The Army response to this effort may include the formation of a medical task force or the deployment of specialized expertise. The Army medical response to disasters is typically provided through special medical augmentation response teams organized by the U.S. Army Medical Command and its subordinate commands, on a task-organized basis, from various worldwide assets. Larger events might require a functional task force, such as a medical task force to conduct medical evacuation, triage, treatment, and public health and medical surveillance.

3-67. DOD may have to augment civil air space management assets and capabilities when their effectiveness has been so significantly degraded that the probability of a catastrophic aviation event is probable. The air component command to the USNORTHCOM has the primary capabilities to provide support to civil aviation, while deconflicting the complexities of operations involving air assets from multiple organizations.

3-68. Soldiers engaged in civil support operations may face threats from criminals, disease, the weather, or TIM. The tasks of safety, FHP (preventive medicine), AT, and CBRN defense are critical considerations for protecting deployed personnel and assets. An accurate, on-going assessment of risk is vital in determining whether and how the deployed commander will provide DSCA.

3-69. Chairman of the Joint Chiefs of Staff Instruction (CJCSI) 3121.01B establishes fundamental policies and procedures governing the actions taken by U.S. commanders and their forces during all DOD civil support and routine military department functions occurring within U.S. territory and territorial seas. During DSCA operations, the Secretary of Defense retains the authority to set the arming level for Title 10 forces. When DOD forces under DOD control operate in coordination with other federal agencies, the applicable rules for the use of force will be coordinated with on-scene federal agency personnel. Standing rules for the use of force also apply to homeland defense missions occurring within U.S. territories. Commanders at all levels are responsible for training their personnel to understand and properly utilize the standing rules for the use of force.

Chapter 4

Protection Integration in Army Operations

This chapter discusses how protection is integrated throughout the operations process. It describes how commanders integrate protection during planning, preparation, execution, and assessment. This chapter also details how the protection cell staff reduces friendly vulnerabilities while developing protection strategies through the application of protection capabilities based on the commander's protection priorities.

OPERATIONS PROCESS

4-1. While each operation differs in design and circumstances, all operations follow a general cycle known as the "operations process." This process consists of the major C2 activities performed during operations—planning, preparation, execution, and continuous assessment. (See figure 4-1.) Doctrine describes this framework by each operations process activity; however, planning, preparing, executing, and assessing occur sequentially or simultaneously.

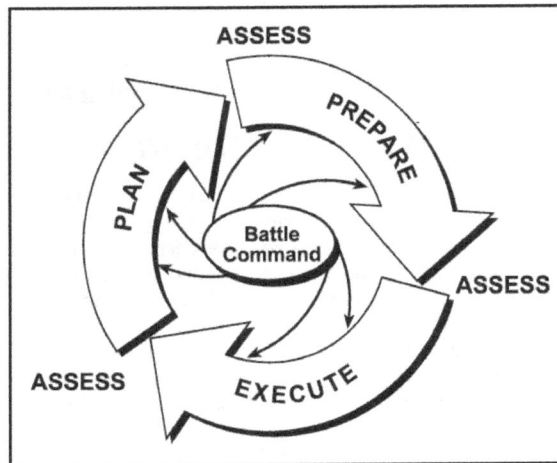

Figure 4-1. Operations process

4-2. During planning, commanders use the MDMP to analyze the mission while translating organizational capabilities in terms of the warfighting functions for integration and expression in a plan or order. Various activities and processes are used during preparation and execution for synchronization and are monitored and evaluated during a process of continual assessment that facilitates decisionmaking.

4-3. Throughout the operations process, commanders accomplish the mission by using several mechanisms to facilitate the integration and synchronization of tasks and functions. Battle rhythm is one key control measure that helps manage the deliberate integration of functions and activities. Army doctrine also illustrates several continuing activities and processes that are used for functional integration in the operations process. For example, terrain management is a continuing activity that relies on the intelligence preparation of the battlefield (IPB) process for its integration and synchronization. These activities and processes occur during all operations and must be synchronized with each other and integrated into the overall operation. (See figure 4-2.) This is often accomplished through the use of cross-functional teams, working groups, and boards.

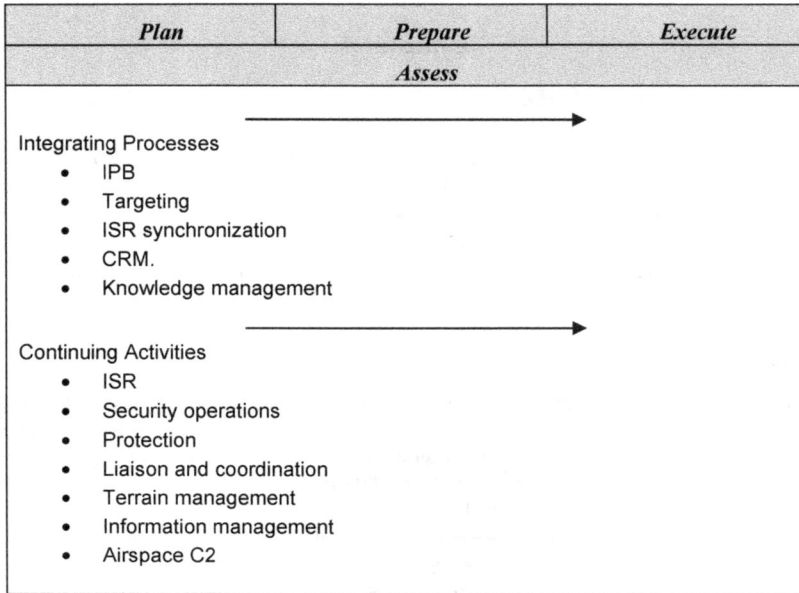

Plan	Prepare	Execute
Assess		

Integrating Processes
- IPB
- Targeting
- ISR synchronization
- CRM.
- Knowledge management

Continuing Activities
- ISR
- Security operations
- Protection
- Liaison and coordination
- Terrain management
- Information management
- Airspace C2

Figure 4-2. Continuing activities and integrating processes

BATTLE COMMAND AND PROTECTION STRATEGIES

4-4.   Commanders drive the operations process through the application of *battle command*, which is the art and science of understanding, visualizing, describing, directing, leading, and assessing forces to impose the commander's will on a hostile, thinking, and adaptive enemy. Battle command applies leadership to translate decisions into actions—by synchronizing forces and warfighting functions in time, space, and purpose—to accomplish missions. (FM 3-0) (See figure 4-3.) Commanders combine the military art and science to translate information and experience into superior decisions faster than the enemy. They also determine priorities, provide guidance, establish time horizons, create command climates, and accept risk in ways that are clear and help focus the staff and subordinate organizations. The commander's inherent responsibility to protect and preserve the force, while seeking every opportunity to act decisively, makes it imperative to consider protection in the operations process.

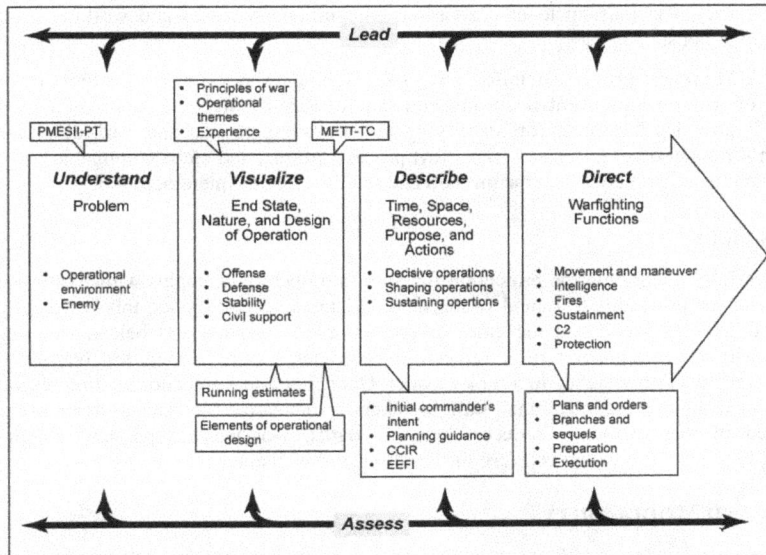

Figure 4-3. Battle command

4-5.   Commanders understand and broadly visualize protection considerations and opportunities in relation to the mission and the OE in terms of the forms of protection. They discern hazards that are preventable and divide threats into those that may be deterred and those that may require the application of security or defensive measures to achieve protection. Commanders provide guidance on risk tolerance, CCIR, and asset or capability criticality to help focus the staff and subordinate leadership.

4-6.   A commander's tolerance for risk may vary with the nature of the threat, operational theme, environmental conditions, or external factors. Leaders always protect all military personnel. All military resources have value, but all military assets are not linked to mission accomplishment in the same manner or at the same time. As the competition for protection assets increases, commanders must provide a clear intent and guidance on where, when, and how much risk they are willing to assume or tolerate. The CRM process provides a context for risk assessment to support decisionmaking. Decision support tools and systems may be helpful within the assessment process to help commanders differentiate between important assets and mission-critical assets.

4-7.   The operations staff assists the commander in integrating protection with the other warfighting functions throughout the operations process. At division and higher levels, the protection cell—

● Focuses effort in the MDMP to produce a plan or order.

● Develops protection strategies to effectively use resources in support of a protection concept of operations.

● Contributes to IPB and situational understanding.

● Identifies vulnerabilities, hazards, and gaps in information.

● Participates in the targeting process and the ISR synchronization process.

● Coordinates with various working groups to further synchronize protection with the other warfighting functions according to the commander's intent and concept of operations.

4-8.   As a continuing activity, protection information and considerations are typically integrated into the operations process by the operations officer using the CRM integrating process. (See FM 5-19 for more information.) The protection cell uses the CRM process to identify, evaluate, and monitor threats and hazards as they emerge, while conducting the functional tasks and monitoring the systems that comprise the protection warfighting function. When leaders employ the CRM process to integrate key protection tasks and systems, they also participate in the various integrating processes and working groups during the conduct of operations.

4-9. The CRM process provides a uniform way of assigning a risk value to an activity by determining the probability of a hazardous event occurring and the severity or outcome in relation to the mission or personnel. It provides a context for identifying and assessing threats and hazards and is a source of information for many other processes. The CRM process informs and alerts commanders to conditions and activities that may negatively affect the mission and require an adjustment decision.

PROTECTION CELL

4-10. Successfully integrating the protection function into operations begins with fixing responsibility for the many disparate protection tasks and systems. At division level and higher, this is typically done through a designated protection cell and the chief of protection. At brigade and below, this may occur more informally with the designation of a protection coordinator from among the brigade staff or as an integrating staff function assigned to a senior leader. Once functional and coordinating responsibilities have been delineated among organizational staff members, protection tasks and systems are integrated and synchronized in the operations process through boards, working groups, and meetings like other warfighting functions. Protection cells are further discussed in chapter 5.

PROTECTION AND MODULARITY

4-11. Brigade combat teams (BCTs), functional brigades, and support brigades perform protection tasks and functions directed by higher headquarters. Brigades incorporate their efforts into an established protection framework developed by the staff at higher headquarters. Among the Army's modular support brigades, the MEB presents a new capability that is ideally suited to perform protection tasks and functions for a division, corps, or multinational force. The MEB can be task-organized as needed to provide the protection requirements needed at division and corps levels. At these levels, the protection cell may recommend the task organization of units whose primary mission is protection. Task organization is the temporary reorganization of the force by using command and support relationships, including a recommended task organization for the MEB and other functional units as required. MEBs are designed to C2 the following units that provide protection and other support to the force:

* Engineer.
* Military police.
* CBRN.
* CA.
* Air defense artillery.
* EOD.
* TCF.

When protection requirements exceed the capabilities of the MEB, the protection cell can identify the need for a functional brigade headquarters. (See figure 4-4.)

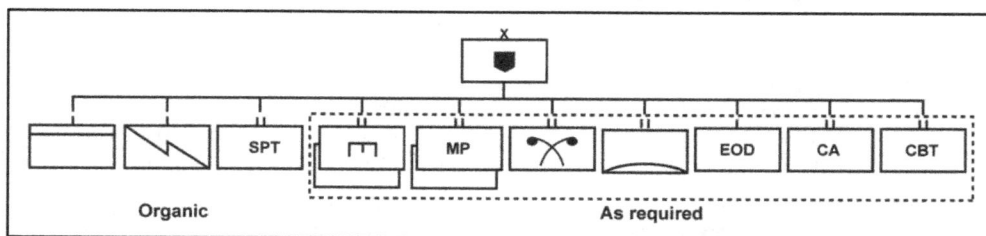

Figure 4-4. MEB task-organized for protection tasks

4-12. The protection cell translates protection guidance and capabilities and the results of analysis into protection strategies using various decision support and analytical tools and the principles of protection. The use of protection principles in developing protection strategies provides coherence to the many diverse and overlapping protection activities and forms existing or occurring in the OE. Commanders at all levels allocate resources to support protection strategies based on an accurate and continual assessment of threats and hazards over time, but remain flexible enough to respond to variances and opportunities and to make adjustments.

PROTECTION AND THE OPERATIONS PROCESS

4-13. The operations process is composed of several supporting topics that further illustrate the activities and tasks necessary to conduct Army operations. For example, the MDMP and orders production support planning, while activities such as reconnaissance and rehearsals support preparation. Decisionmaking characterizes execution and is necessary to direct the application of combat power and to synchronize activities. While assessment occurs continuously throughout the operations process to provide situational understanding, monitoring and evaluating additional assessments also occur specifically to planning, preparing, and executing operations. (See table 4-1.)

Table 4-1. Expanded operations process with supporting topics

Plan	Prepare	Execute

• TLP and MDMP
• Plans and orders
	• Reconnaissance
	• Security
	• Force protection
	• Plan revision and refinement
	• Coordination and liaison
	• Rehearsals
	• Task organization
	• Training
	• Movement
	• Precombat checks and inspections
	• Integration of new Soldiers and units
		• Decide
		  ▪ Execution
		  ▪ Adjustment
		• Direct
		  ▪ Apply combat power
		  ▪ Synchronize
		  ▪ Maintain continuity

Assessment During Planning	**Assessment During Preparation**	**Assessment During Execution**
• Monitor the situation • Monitor MOP/MOE • Evaluate COAs	• Monitor preparations • Evaluate preparations	• Monitor operations • Evaluate progress
Continuous Assessment		
• Situational understanding—sources, solutions • Monitoring—situation/operations, MOP/MOE • Evaluating—forecast, seize, retain, and exploit the initiative; variances		

4-14. While each protection task and system has its own operational consideration, each must be synchronized within a coherent protection strategy or concept to ensure synergistic protection efforts. For example, AMD without survivability is much less effective. Area security without AT, OPSEC, and physical security is also less effective. To ensure this synergy, the protection cell develops protection strategies around which MOP and MOE can be established. In this way, the success or failure of each individual protection effort can be monitored and evaluated.

Note. Chapter 2 discusses protection tasks and systems.

CONTINUOUS ASSESSMENT

4-15. *Assessment* is the continuous monitoring and evaluation of the current situation, particularly the enemy, and progress of an operation. (FM 3-0) Commanders typically base assessments on their situational understanding, which is generally a composite of several informational sources and intuition. Staff members normally develop running estimates that illustrate the significant aspects of a particular activity or function over time. These estimates are used by commanders to maintain situational awareness and direct adjustments. Significant changes or variances among or within running estimates can signal a threat or an opportunity, alerting commanders to take action.

4-16. Assessing protection is an essential, continuing activity that occurs throughout the operations process. While a failure in protection is typically easy to detect, the successful application of protection may be difficult to assess and quantify. For example, although prevention and deterrence may consume significant resources that are easy to quantify, the absence of accidents or threat actions does not necessarily mean that the plan is working or that leaders are managing risk well. This makes the measured assessment of deliberate protection activities essential to determining the effectiveness of the plan, task organization, or operational concept.

4-17. Deliberate assessment is enabled by monitoring and evaluating criteria derived from the tasks and systems that comprise the protection warfighting function. Criteria used to monitor and evaluate the situation or operation may be represented as MOP or MOE. These measures are discrete, relevant, and responsive benchmarks that are useful in all operations. They may contain the CCIR and EEFI and may generate information requirements. MOP and MOE can be significant decision support tools and may drive transition periods, resource allocations, and other critical decisions.

Measure of Performance

4-18. A MOP helps determine whether a commander has applied enough, correct resources to an operation. A *MOP* is a criterion used to assess friendly actions and that is tied to measuring task accomplishment. (JP 3-0) This measure is friendly force-oriented. It measures task accomplishment; and in its simplest form, it answers whether a task was performed successfully. FM 7-15 provides a table with MOPs that can be used to develop standards for each task. Some specific MOPs may be altered for their relevance to the local situation or they may be omitted; however, all changes to established MOPs should be disseminated vertically and horizontally among headquarters and participants in an operation or activity.

Measure of Effectiveness

4-19. A MOE is useful in determining success and deciding whether a commander must maintain, adjust, or reallocate resources. An *MOE* is a criterion used to assess changes in system behavior, capability, or OE that is tied to measuring the attainment of an end state, achievement of an objective, or creation of an effect. (JP 3-0) It is oriented to mission accomplishment, focuses on the results or consequences of an action, and is used to assess changes in the OE. This is more often a subjective assessment as it tends to measure long-term results. As a result, an MOE may consist of a series of indicators that are used to judge success or failure.

4-20. Significant changes in some environmental conditions are subtle and only occur over a long period of time, yet protection activities must be continual. The enduring nature of protection could cause complacency or inattentiveness, requiring leaders to stay focused on determining, monitoring, and evaluating accurate protection indicators and warnings that maintain situational understanding and alert them to risk.

4-21. Commanders monitor MOEs and evaluate variances and change indicators for cause and effect to forecast failure or identify a critical point of failure in an activity or operation. Based on this type of assessment, resources can be reassigned to mitigate the overall risk to the mission or to support or reinforce specific local security efforts. The goal is to anticipate the need for action before failure occurs, rather than react to an unplanned loss. Thorough staff planning in the MDMP allows commanders to accelerate decisionmaking by preplanning responses to anticipated events through the use of battle drills, branches, and sequels. War-gaming critical events also allows commanders to focus their CCIR and the supporting information collection effort. Information developed during this process can be used to develop EEFI and indicators or warnings that relate to the development of protection priorities.

4-22. If an action appears to be failing in its desired effect, the result may be attributed to—
- Personnel or equipment system failure.
- Insufficient resource allocation at vulnerable points.

- Variance in anticipated threat combat power ratio, resulting in an increased risk equation.
- Ineffective supporting efforts, leading to a cumulative failure of more critical elements.

4-23. Assessment identifies the magnitude and significance of variances in performance or conditions from those that were expected through prior forecasting to determine if an adjustment decision is needed. Commanders monitor the ongoing operation to determine if it is progressing satisfactorily according to the current plan, including fragmentary orders that have modified it. The staff assesses the situation in relation to established protection criteria. This assessment ensures that facts and assumptions remain valid and also identifies new facts and assumptions. Assessment decreases reaction time by anticipating future requirements and linking them to current plans.

Critical Asset List

4-24. **The *critical asset list (CAL)* is a prioritized list of assets that should be protected; it is normally identified by the phase of an operation and approved by the commander.** Once the threat, criticality, and vulnerability assessments are complete, the staff presents the prioritized list of critical assets to the commander for approval. Commanders typically operate in a resource-constrained environment and have a finite amount of combat power for protecting assets. Therefore, the protection cell determines which assets are critical for mission success and recommends protection priorities based on the available resources. The list will vary depending on the mission variables.

4-25. During threat assessment, members of the protection cell identify and prioritize the commander's critical assets using the vulnerability assessment, criticality assessment, and plan or order. Critical assets are generally specific assets of such extraordinary importance that their loss or degradation would have a significant and debilitating effect on operations or the mission. (See JP 3-07.2 for more information.) They represent what "should" be protected. The protection cell and working group use information derived from command guidance, IPB, warning orders, and the restated mission to nominate critical assets from their particular protection functional area. Vulnerability and criticality assessments are generally intended to be sequential. However, the criticality assessment can be conducted before, after, or concurrent with threat assessments. The vulnerability assessment should be conducted after the threat and criticality assessments to orient protection efforts on the most important assets. These assessments provide the staff with data to develop benchmarks, running estimates, CCIR, change indicators, variances, and MOP/MOE.

4-26. This lack of replacement may then cause that critical asset to become the first priority for protection. Not all assets listed on the CAL will receive protection from continuously applied combat power. Critical assets with some protection from applied combat power become part of the defended asset list (DAL).

4-27. CAL development may require the establishment of evaluation criteria, such as value (impact of loss), depth (proximity in distance and time), replacement impact (degree of effort, cost, or time), and capability (function and capacity for current and future operations). (See figure 4-5, page 4-8.)

Defended Asset List

4-28. When compared to the assessed threats, the vulnerability and criticality assessments provide the commander with information to make decisions about which assets are the most critical, which assets must have combat power dedicated to their protection, and where he can accept risk. For instance, one of five critical assets considered in a given criticality assessment cannot be replaced during an operation, while the other four can. This lack of replacement or recuperation may cause that critical asset to become the first priority for protection. Not all assets listed on the CAL will receive deliberate protection reinforcement. Some assets will derive additional protection from the complementary effect of other ongoing warfighting functions, while remaining assets may rely on organic security measures and self-protection. Critical assets that are reinforced with additional protection capabilities or capabilities from other combat power elements become part of the DAL. **The *DAL* is a listing of those assets from the CAL, prioritized by the commander, to be defended with the resources available.** It represents what "can" be protected, by priority. This allows the commander to apply finite protection capabilities to the most valuable assets. The combat power applied may be a weapon system, electronic sensor, obstacle, or combination. The CAL and DAL are dynamic lists (see figure 4-6, page 4-8).

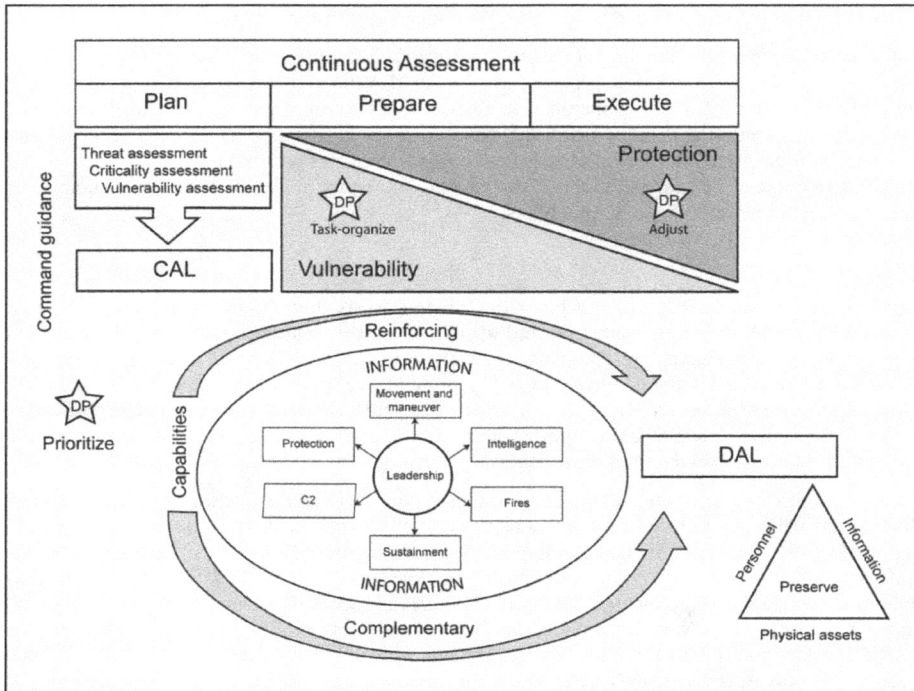

Figure 4-5. CAL and DAL in the operations process

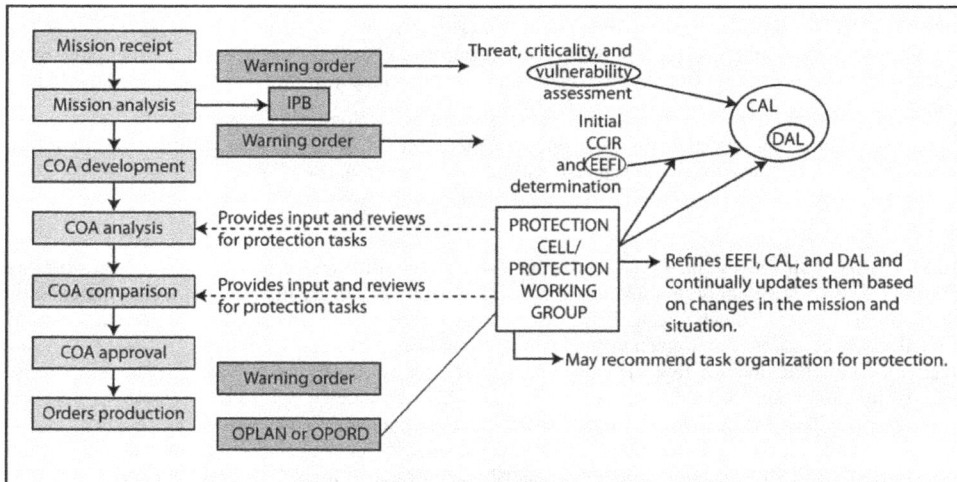

Figure 4-6. Protection cell and planning process

4-29. Assessment permits the commander to shape protection measures and provides valuable information for refining future protection activities. Commanders stay alert to transitions in operations. Significant changes in the situation and environment often affect vulnerabilities to the force; such changes may require adjustments to CALs and DALs.

4-30. Commanders and units remain flexible while conducting protection operations. When the situation changes significantly, the protection plan must be adapted so that resources and opportunities are not wasted. Commanders should not hesitate to modify the protection plan if it fails to adequately protect critical assets.

4-31. The most important question when assessing the effectiveness of applied protection capabilities is whether the allocation of resources and combat power to protection tasks remain valid. The staff compares expectations to actual events to determine the overall effectiveness of the plan, and they recommend appropriate adjustments. They answer the following questions:

- Was the plan successful?
- Were the assets protected?
- Were Soldiers accidentally killed or injured?
- Were the correct assets defended?
- Did protection equipment or TTP fail?
- What actions must be taken to restore critical capabilities or mitigate damage?
- Is it necessary to reallocate assets because of enemy actions?
- What protection assets are available for reinforcement?
- What activities can be combined to produce a complementary protective effect?
- What additional protection capabilities are needed?
- What current protection capabilities are not needed?

4-32. Commanders must prepare for success and failure when planning to mitigate the risk to the mission and force. A significant change in the situation may represent successful mission accomplishment. However, commanders can become vulnerable or complacent immediately after mission accomplishment due to fatigue or exuberance arising from victory. As the chance of human error increases, an unprepared force becomes vulnerable to enemy counterattacks or surprise attacks.

4-33. Since many protection information requirements are long-term and overlap staff functions, the protection cell often develops a means of quantifying progress and normal activities. In planning, the staff develops specific information requirements oriented on protection. These requirements may be represented as CCIR and used to focus collection efforts or as change indicators to alert or measure variances in baseline assumptions detailed in the protection concept of operation. Protection effectiveness, progress, and success can be expressed in many ways—including the reaction time of response forces; duration of specific, uninterrupted military capabilities; statistics on Soldiers returned to duty; and many others.

4-34. The criteria used to evaluate the degree of mission success can be expressed as—

- MOP to determine how well protection tasks achieved the intended purpose.
- MOE to evaluate the overall effectiveness of protection plans and assumptions.

PLANNING

4-35. Planning is the first step toward effective protection. Commanders consider the most likely threats and decide which personnel, physical assets, and information to protect. They set protection priorities for each phase or critical event of an operation. The MDMP or troop-leading procedures provide a deliberate process and context to develop and examine information for use in the various continuing activities and integrating processes that comprise the operations process. Effective protection strategies and risk decisions are developed based on information that flows from mission analysis, allowing a thorough understanding of the situation, mission, and environment. Mission analysis typically occurs during planning, and the CRM process provides a context to identify and analyze threats and hazards before their integration in preparation and execution. (See table 4-2, page 4-10.)

Note. See FM 5-19 for more information on CRM and MDMP.

Table 4-2. CRM process

MDMP Steps	Risk Management Steps				
	Step 1. Identify Hazards	Step 2. Assess Hazards	Step 3. Develop Controls and Make Risk Decisions	Step 4. Implement Controls	Step 5. Supervise and Evaluate
Mission receipt	X				
Mission analysis	X	X			
COA development	X	X	X		
COA analysis	X	X	X		
COA comparison			X		
COA approval			X		
Orders production			X	X	
Rehearsal	X	X	X	X	X
Execution/assessment	X	X	X	X	X

4-36. During mission analysis, functional proponents in the protection cell develop running estimates of their specific protection task and system that are used to monitor and evaluate protection efforts throughout the operations process. These estimates can be used to develop variances and their change indicators from which MOP and MOE may be further developed.

Planning Guidance

4-37. Planners receive guidance as commanders describe their visualization of the operational concept and intent. This guidance generally focuses on COA development by identifying decisive and supporting efforts, massing effects, and stating priorities. Effective planning guidance provides a broad perspective of the commander's visualization with the latitude to explore additional options. Command guidance is often issued using the warfighting functions as criterion. A commander's initial protection guidance may include—

- Protection priorities.
- Work priorities for survivability assets.
- AMD positioning guidance.
- Specific terrain and weather factors.
- Intelligence focus and limitations for security efforts.
- Areas or events where risk is acceptable.
- Protected targets and areas.
- Vehicle and equipment safety or security constraints.
- PR C2.
- FPCON status.
- FHP measures.
- MOPP guidance.
- Environmental guidance.
- INFOCON.
- UXO guidance.
- OPSEC risk tolerance.
- ROE, standing rules for the use of force, and rules of interaction.
- Escalation of force and nonlethal weapons guidance.

4-38. Commanders typically determine their own CCIR, but may select some from staff nominations. Staff sections recommend the most important priority intelligence requirements (PIR) and friendly force information requirements for the commander to designate as CCIR.

Plans and Orders

4-39. The approved vulnerability reduction mitigation measures, commander's decisions for acceptable risks, CAL, and DAL represent running estimates that are incorporated into appropriate plans and orders. Based on these estimates, the protection cell develops the concept of protection in the base order and appropriate annexes.

4-40. Protection strategies are developed after receiving guidance and considering the forms and principles of protection in relation to the mission variables and the tasks and systems that comprise the protection warfighting function. The concept of protection is based on the mission variables and should include protection priorities by area, unit, activity, or resource. It should also address how protection can be applied and derived during the conduct of operations. For example, the security for routes, bases, and critical infrastructure can be accomplished by applying protection assets in dedicated, fixed, or local security roles; or it may be derived from economy-of-force protection measures such as area security techniques. It also identifies areas and conditions where forces may become fixed or static and unable to derive protection from their ability to maneuver and press the offensive. These conditions, areas, or situations are anticipated; and the associated risks are mitigated by describing and planning for the use of TCFs and other response forces.

4-41. Planners integrate protection actions and information throughout specific plans and orders. Some significant, protection-related products that are often produced in the planning process include the—

- Protection concept or strategy that supports and nests with the operational concept.
- Running estimate that reflects protection tasks and systems.
- Quantifiable level of risk for specific events and activities.
- Protection MOP and MOE and threshold variances.
- Recommendations for CCIR that reflect decision criteria from protection tasks and systems.
- CAL and DAL.
- Decision points (DP) based on the commander's risk tolerance level.

4-42. Information protection is part of the protection warfighting function; and because it involves procedural and technical instructions related to information systems (including networks), it is typically addressed within the NETOPS section of most plans and orders. FHP is included in the health service support section. The G-6/signal staff officer (S-6) and echelon surgeon coordinate their input to plans and orders with the chief of protection.

4-43. Although protection is continuous and enduring, many operations are not. This makes efficient protection planning difficult and dependent on clear command guidance. Long planning horizons may permit increasingly detailed analysis in the development of some plans and orders or in the assessments they contain, while other situations afford only hasty methods. For example, protection planning often requires criticality, vulnerability, or recuperability analysis. Commanders must weigh the benefit that a potentially lengthy protection analysis provides when compared with less accurate, hasty methods.

ASSESSMENT DURING PLANNING

4-44. The continuous assessment that occurs during planning includes activities that are necessary to maintain situational understanding and those that continue to monitor and evaluate running estimates, MOEs, and MOPs; identify variances; and support decisionmaking. These assessment activities are consistent throughout all parts of the operations process. However, certain assessments occur during planning that are specific to the planning process, MDMP, or mission analysis. For example, the protection cell evaluates COA during MDMP against evaluation criteria derived from the protection warfighting function to determine if each COA is feasible, acceptable, or suitable in relation to its ability to protect or preserve the force.

4-45. The staff may also conduct a specific analysis to assess threat capability or the vulnerability and criticality of an asset to assist commanders in determining protection priorities or task organization decisions. This type of analysis is often required when the nature of the operation is enduring or requires a continuous, dedicated protection effort or when the potential loss of the protected asset has significant consequences.

Threat and Hazard Assessment

4-46. Threats include hazards with the potential to cause injury, illness, or death of personnel; damage to or loss of equipment or property; or mission degradation. Commanders and protection cell staff are concerned with three general categories of threats:

- **Hostile actions.** Threats from hostile actions include any capability that enemy forces or criminal elements have to inflict damage upon personnel, physical assets, or information. These threats may include IEDs, suicide bombings, network attacks, mortars, asset theft, air attacks, or CBRNE weapons.
- **Nonhostile activities.** Threats from nonhostile activities include hazards associated with Soldier duties within their occupational specialty, Soldier activity while off duty, and unintentional actions that cause harm. Examples include on- and off-duty accidents, OPSEC violations, network compromises, equipment malfunctions, or accidental CBRNE incidents.
- **Environmental conditions.** Environmental threats are hazards associated with the surrounding environment that could potentially degrade readiness or mission accomplishment. Weather, natural disasters, and disease are common examples. The protection cell staff also considers how military operations may affect noncombatants in the AO. Such considerations prevent unnecessary collateral damage and regard how civilians (those merely going about their day-to-day activities) will affect the mission. Heavy civilian vehicle or pedestrian traffic adversely affects convoys and other operations.

4-47. Commanders use the following METT-TC mission variables to describe the OE, including threats that may impact protection:

- **Mission.** The nature of the operational mission may imply specific hazards. Some missions are inherently more dangerous than others. Leaders look for hazards associated with the complexity of higher headquarters plans and orders, such as a particularly complex scheme of maneuver. Using a fragmentary order in lieu of a detailed operation plan (OPLAN) or operation order (OPORD) raises the vulnerability because of possible misunderstanding. Since protection is a continuing activity, leaders also look for hazards in on- and off-duty garrison activities.
- **Enemy.** Commanders try to determine the enemy's capability and intent that pose threats to the operation or mission. During planning, the protection staff participates in the IPB process. IPB is a dynamic staff process that is critical to identifying enemy threats. IPB supports threat-based risk assessments by identifying opportunities and constraints that the OE offers to enemy and friendly forces. It also portrays a picture of enemy capabilities and vulnerabilities. In the on- and off-duty garrison environment, enemy considerations take the form of outside influences that may affect or impact a planned event or activity.
- **Terrain and weather**. To identify and access terrain-related hazards that can impact force protection or preservation and affect operations, leaders use the military aspects of terrain—observation and fields of fire, avenues of approach, key terrain, obstacles, and cover and concealment (OAKOC). Predeployment checklists are useful in making assessments associated with nonmission activities. Common terrain hazards are elevation, altitude, road surfaces, curves, grades, and traffic density. To assess common weather hazards, leaders use the military aspects of weather (precipitation, temperature and humidity, visibility, winds, and clouds). Illumination may also be a factor of risk assessment. Whether planning a PR operation or out-of-town leave, terrain and weather can create specific hazards. Leaders assess these mission variables for all activities.
- **Troops and support available.** Leaders consider hazards associated with the level of training, staffing, and equipment maintenance and condition. These hazards affect morale and the availability of supplies and services, including the physical, spiritual, and behavioral health of

Soldiers. For nonmission activities, troops include Soldiers, their dependents, civilian workers, and others, whether or not they are connected to the activity. Some examples of other-than-mission hazards include sexual assault, domestic violence, substance abuse, sexually transmitted diseases, and other behavioral or medical conditions.

- **Time available.** Insufficient time for mission preparation often forces commanders to accept greater risk when planning, preparing, and executing plans and orders associated with mission planning. To avoid or mitigate the risks associated with inadequate time for planning, leaders should allow subordinates two-thirds of the available planning time as a control measure. For nonmission activities, insufficient time is a matter of haste rather than availability. This especially applies during holiday periods when the zeal of young Soldiers to get home may lead them to depart duty stations without sufficient rest.

- **Civil considerations.** This variable expands the consideration of hazards to include those that a tactical mission may pose to the civilian populace and noncombatants in the AO. The objective is to reduce collateral damage to civilians and noncombatants. Hazards are also created by the presence of a large civilian population and their efforts to conduct day-to-day living during the course of a mission. Dense civilian traffic may present hazards to convoys and maneuver schemes. Such diverse elements as insurgents, riots, and criminal activity must also be assessed. For nonmission activities, the term addresses those legal, regulatory, or policy considerations that may impact a desired activity or limit a COA.

Criticality Assessment

4-48. A criticality assessment identifies key assets that are required to accomplish a mission. It addresses the impact of temporary or permanent loss of key assets or unit ability to conduct a mission. It examines costs of recovery and reconstitution, including time, expense, capability, and infrastructure support. The staff gauges how quickly a lost capability can be replaced before giving an accurate status to the commander. The general sequence for a criticality assessment is—

- List the key assets and capabilities.
- Determine if critical functions or combat power can be substantially duplicated with other elements of the command or an external resource.
- Determine the time required to substantially duplicate key assets and capabilities in the event of temporary or permanent loss.
- Set priorities for response to threats toward personnel, physical assets, and information.

4-49. The protection cell staff continuously updates the criticality assessment during the operations process. As the staff develops or modifies a friendly COA, ISR efforts confirm or deny information requirements. As the mission or threat changes, initial criticality assessments may also change, increasing or decreasing the subsequent force vulnerability. The protection cell monitors and evaluates these changes and begins coordination among the staff to implement modifications to the protection concept or recommends new protection priorities. PIR, running estimates, MOPs, and MOEs, are continually updated and adjusted to reflect the current and anticipated risks associated with the OE.

Vulnerability Assessment

4-50. A *vulnerability assessment* is a DOD, command, or unit level evaluation (assessment) to determine the vulnerability of a terrorist attack against an installation, unit, exercise, port, ship, residence, facility, or other site. (JP 3-07.2) It identifies areas of improvement to withstand, mitigate, or deter acts of violence or terrorism. The staff addresses the questions of "who" or "what" is vulnerable and "how" it is vulnerable. The vulnerability assessment identifies physical characteristics or procedures that render critical assets, areas, infrastructures, or special events vulnerable to known or potential threats and hazards. The assessment provides a basis for developing controls to eliminate or mitigate vulnerabilities. Vulnerability is the component of risk over which the commander has the most control and greatest influence. The general sequence of a vulnerability assessment is—

- List assets and capabilities and the threats against them.
- Determine common criteria for assessing vulnerabilities.
- Evaluate the assets and capabilities for their vulnerability.

4-51. Vulnerability evaluation criteria may include the degree to which an asset may be disrupted, quantity available (if replacement is required due to loss), dispersion (geographic proximity), and key physical characteristics as required.

4-52. DOD has created several decision support tools to perform criticality assessments in support of the vulnerability assessment process (including mission, symbolism, history, accessibility, recognizability, population, and proximity [MSHARPP] and criticality, accessibility, recuperability, vulnerability, effect, and recognizability [CARVER]). Protection cells can use any of these tools.

> *Note.* DOD O-2000.12-H discusses MSHARPP and CARVER in detail.

Protection Priorities

4-53. Although all military assets are important and all resources have value, the capabilities they represent share no inherent equality in their contribution to decisive operations or overall mission accomplishment. Determining and directing protection priorities may be the most important decisions that commanders make and staffs support. There are seldom sufficient resources to simultaneously provide all assets the same level of protection. For this reason, commanders use CRM to identify increasingly risky activities and events, while other decision support tools assist in prioritizing protection resources.

4-54. Most prioritization methodologies assist in differentiating what is important from what is urgent. In protection planning, the challenge is to differentiate between critical assets and important assets and further determine what protection is possible with available protection capabilities. Event-driven operations may be short in duration, enabling a formidable protection posture for a short time; condition-driven operations may be open-ended and long-term, requiring an enduring and sustainable protection strategy. In either situation, commanders must provide guidance on prioritizing protection capabilities and categorizing important assets.

4-55. Initial protection planning requires various assessments to support protection prioritization; namely, threat, vulnerability, and criticality assessments. These assessments are used to determine which assets can be protected given no constraints (critical assets) and which assets can be protected with available resources (defended assets). Commanders make decisions on acceptable risks and provide guidance to the staff so that they can employ protection capabilities based on the CAL and DAL. All forms of protection are utilized and employed during preparation and continue through execution to reduce friendly vulnerability.

PREPARATION

4-56. *Preparation* consists of activities by the unit before execution to improve ability to conduct the operation, including, but not limited to, the following: plan refinement; rehearsals; reconnaissance, coordination, inspection, and movement. (FM 3-0)

4-57. Preparation includes increased application and/or emphasis on active and passive protection measures. During preparation, the protection cell may conduct or coordinate the following activities:
- Revising and refining the plan.
- Emplacing systems to detect threats to the CAL.
- Directing OPSEC measures.
- Designating quick-reaction forces or TCFs and troop movements.
- Preparing and improving survivability positions.
- Liaising and coordinating with adjacent and protected units.
- Determining indicators and warnings for ISR operations.
- Rehearsing.
- Training with defended assets.
- Confirming subordinate back briefs.
- Implementing vulnerability reduction measures.

4-58. During preparation, the protection cell ensures that the controls or risk reduction measures developed during planning have been implemented and are reflected in plans, SOPs, and running estimates, even as the threat assessment is continuously updated. New threats and hazards are identified or anticipated based on newly assessed threat capabilities or changes in environmental conditions as compared with known friendly vulnerabilities and weaknesses. Commanders use after-action reviews and war games to identify changes to the threat. The protection cell and working group maintain a list of prioritized threats, adverse conditions, and hazard causes. The challenge is to find the root cause or nature of a threat or hazard so that the most effective protection solution can be implemented and disseminated.

4-59. As the staff monitors and evaluates the performance or effectiveness of friendly COA, reconnaissance collects information that may confirm or deny forecasted threat COAs. As the threat changes, risk to the force changes. Some changes may require a different protection posture or the implementation or cessation of specific protection measures and activities. The protection cell analyzes changes or variances that may require modifications to protection priorities and obtains guidance when necessary. Threat assessment is a dynamic and continually changing process. Chiefs of protection and planners stay alert for changing indicators and warnings in the OE that would signal new or fluctuating threats and hazards.

4-60. Complete intelligence for a specific threat assessment is seldom available. Changes in the situation often dictate adjustments or changes to the plan when they exceed variance thresholds established in planning. During preparation, the staff continues to monitor and evaluate the overall situation because variable threat assessment information may generate new PIR, while changes in asset criticality could lead to new friendly force information requirements. Updated critical information requirements could be required based on changes to asset vulnerability and criticality when conjoined with the threat assessment.

4-61. Commanders exercising battle command direct and lead throughout the entire operations process as they provide supervision in concert with the CRM process. Commanders' actions during preparation may also include—

- Reconciling the threat assessment with personal judgment and experience.
- Providing guidance on risk tolerance and making risk decisions.
- Emphasizing protection tasks and systems during rehearsals.
- Minimizing unnecessary interference with subunits to allow maximum preparatory time.
- Circulating throughout the environment to observe precombat inspections.
- Directing control measures to reduce risks associated with preparatory movement.
- Expediting the procurement and availability of resources needed for protection implementation.
- Requesting higher headquarters support to reinforce logistical preparations and replenishment.

4-62. Depending on the situation and the threat, some protection tasks may be conducted for short or long durations, covering the course of several missions or an entire operation. The staff coordinates the commander's protection priorities with vulnerability mitigation measures and clearly communicates them to—

- Superior, subordinate, and adjacent units.
- Civilian agencies and personnel that are part of the force or may be impacted by the task or control.

4-63. Subordinate leaders also conduct CRM and provide supervision to ensure that Soldiers understand their responsibilities to and the significance of protection measures, tasks, and systems. This is normally accomplished during mission preparation through training, rehearsals, task organization, and resource allocation. Rehearsals, especially those using opposing force personnel, can provide a measure of protection plan effectiveness. (See FM 3-0 for more information.)

ASSESSMENT DURING PREPARATION

4-64. Although continuous assessment occurs during preparation and includes activities required to maintain situational understanding; monitor and evaluate running estimates, MOE, and MOP; and identify variances for decision support, some assessments are specific to preparatory activities. These assessments generally provide commanders with a composite estimate of preoperational force readiness or status in time to make adjustments.

4-65. During preparation, the protection cell may focus on threats and hazards that can influence preparatory activities, to include monitoring new Soldier integration programs and movement schedules or evaluating live-fire requirements for precombat checks and inspections. The protection cell may evaluate training and rehearsals or provide coordination and liaison to facilitate effectiveness in high risk or complex preparatory activities, such as movement and logistics preparation.

EXECUTION

4-66. *Execution* is putting a plan into action by applying combat power to accomplish the mission and using situational understanding to assess progress and make execution and adjustment decisions. (FM 3-0)

4-67. Commanders exercising battle command decide, direct, and provide leadership to organizations and Soldiers during execution. As operations develop and progress, the commander interprets information that flows from C2 systems for indicators and warnings that signal the need for execution or adjustment decisions. Commanders may direct and redirect the way combat power is applied or preserved and may adjust the tempo of operations through synchronization. The continuous and enduring character of protection activities makes the continuity of protection actions and activities essential during execution. Commanders implement control measures and allocate resources that are sufficient to ensure protection continuity and restoration.

4-68. The protection cell monitors and evaluates several critical ongoing functions associated with execution for operational actions or changes that impact protection cell proponents. Some of these functions include—

- Ensuring that the protection focus supports the decisive operation.
- Reviewing and adjusting the CCIR derived from protection tasks and systems.
- Reviewing changes to graphic control measures and boundaries for the increased risk of fratricide.
- Evaluating the effectiveness of C2 battle tracking for constraints on PR.
- Monitoring the employment of security forces for gaps in protection or unintended patterns.
- Evaluating the effectiveness of liaison personnel for protection activities.
- Evaluating movement coordination and control to protect critical paths.
- Monitoring adjacent unit coordination procedures for terrain management vulnerabilities.
- Monitoring readiness rates of response forces involved in fixed-site protection.
- Monitoring FHP.

4-69. Staff members are also particularly alert for reports and events that meet CCIR. Once a threat to a critical or defended asset is detected by monitoring and evaluating running estimates and MOEs for indicators and warnings, the protection cell alerts the unit responsible for protecting the asset or recommends additional protective action. Unit commanders respond to their assessment of the threat or deliberate warning and then execute contingency or response plans. For example, if a threat force attacks an asset, the commander applies combat power to defeat it. Commanders are alerted by CCIR if the capability of the threat force reflects a variance that exceeds anticipated and projected combat power ratios. They may respond to the increased risk by rendering an execution or adjustment decision to commit additional assets in the form of response forces or fires that are necessary to defeat or neutralize the threat.

4-70. Events frequently occur that prompt commanders to reevaluate assessed threat and vulnerability, usually due to a significant change in the situation. Examples include a change in mission, loss of a critical asset, newly discovered enemy capability, environmental change, political or civil event, or change in the ROE. Commanders must stay as sensitive to the risk calculus as they are to changes in readiness rates or available manpower in terms of immediate combat power. When commanders adjust or change their risk calculation, the process begins anew. The staff compares the new friendly situation to the known enemy situation, develops controls, recommends priorities and DPs, and then implements the decisions. The protection cell determines—

- Where protection assets can best help mission accomplishment with acceptable risk.
- If protection assets should be committed to the mission immediately or be held in reserve.
- If assets should be moved due to a change in the DAL.
- Whether the commander needs to request assistance and, if so, for what purpose.

4-71. There may be a change in the ROE or political, civil, or environmental situation. These unanticipated changes may not require immediate action. However, commanders must consider how changes relate to the mission as they mitigate the vulnerability to civilians and the environment. They must—

- Determine if immediate actions will minimize damage.
- Decide whether actions will affect mission accomplishment.
- Determine if the staff balance requires protective actions.
- Ensure overall mission accomplishment.

ASSESSMENT DURING EXECUTION

4-72. Upon publication of the OPORD, the protection cell and protection working group monitor the situation so that protection tasks approved by the commander are executed according to plan.

4-73. The protection cell monitors and evaluates the progress of current operations to validate assumptions made in planning and to continually update changes to the situation. The protection cell and protection working group continually meet to monitor threats to the CAL and DAL, and they recommend changes to the protection plan as required. They monitor the conduct of operations, looking for variances from the OPORD that affect their areas of expertise. When variances exceed a threshold value developed or directed in planning, the protection cell may recommend an adjustment decision to counter an unforecasted threat or hazard or to mitigate a developing vulnerability. They also track the status of protection assets and evaluate the effectiveness of the protection systems as they are employed. Additionally, the protection cell and protection working group monitor actions of other staff sections by periodically reviewing plans, orders, and risk assessments to determine if those areas require a change in protection priorities, posture, or resource allocation.

LESSONS LEARNED

4-74. The way organizations and Soldiers learn from mistakes is key in protecting the force. Although the evaluation process occurs throughout the operations process, it also occurs as part of the after-action review and assessment following the mission. Leaders at all levels ensure that Soldiers and equipment are combat-ready. Leaders demonstrate their responsibility to sound stewardship practices and risk management principles required to ensure the minimal losses of resources and military assets due to hostile, nonhostile, or environmental threats. Key lessons learned are immediately applied and shared with other commands. Commanders develop systems to ensure the rapid dissemination of approved lessons learned and TTP proven to save lives or protect equipment and information. The protection cells at each command echelon evaluate the integration of lessons learned and constantly coordinate protection lessons with other staff elements within and between the levels of command.

4-75. Postoperational evaluations typically—

- Identify threats that were not identified as part of the initial assessment or identify new threats that evolved during the operation or activity. For example, when personnel, equipment, environment, or mission changes the initial assessments, the control measures are reevaluated.
- Assess effectiveness in supporting operational goals and objectives. For example, determine if the controls positively or negatively impacted training or mission accomplishment and determine if the controls supported existing doctrine and TTP.
- Assess the implementation, execution, and communication of controls.
- Assess the accuracy of residual risk and effectiveness of controls in eliminating hazards and controlling risks.
- Ensure compliance with the guiding principles of CRM.
  - Was the process integrated throughout all phases of the operation?
  - Were risk decisions accurate?
  - Were risk decisions made at the appropriate level?
  - Did any unnecessary risks or benefits outweigh the cost in terms of expense, training benefit, or time?
  - Was the process cyclic and continuous throughout the operation?

Chapter 5

Protection Cells

The protection warfighting function applies to all levels of command. The Army structure provides established protection cells at division level and above. Protection cells are found in main and tactical command posts at division and corps levels and in main or contingency command posts at theater Army headquarters. This chapter uses examples from the modular division design since the protection cells in the modular division and corps closely resemble each other. At the Headquarters DA level, the G-3/assistant chief of staff, civil affairs (G-5)/assistant chief of staff, information engagement (G-7) is the staff agent for the Army protection policy. In order to enhance integration and coordination of all protection-related activities, the Army Oversight Board for Protection serves as the protection cell for the Army. This board is the central source that provides senior leaders with the requisite situational awareness to deconflict efforts, reduce duplication, prioritize areas of focus, and approve new initiatives.

ROLES AND RESPONSIBILITIES

5-1. The protection cell is generally responsible for integrating or coordinating the tasks and systems that fall under the protection warfighting function. Protection cells help craft protection strategies that are reflected in the concept of protection included in the base order and appropriate annexes and appendixes. Some protection tasks, such as FHP and AMD, may also have representation in other operational cells at higher level organizations. At the theater army level, the protection cell may recommend that the commander tailor protective elements when required for the campaign or major operation. Tailoring includes the makeup of the force and the recommended sequence of its deployment. In addition to tailoring force packages, the theater army protection cell—

- Examines other protection plans, concepts, and strategies for insights on survivability, security force employment, task organization, and economy-of-force options.
- Considers multinational and host nation capabilities and determines how to integrate them into protection.
- Determines if other capabilities or disciplines (civil-military activities, information engagement tasks) from within the force can provide complementary or reinforcing capabilities to achieve protection and reduce the likelihood of successful attacks.

5-2. The protection cell advises commanders on the priorities for protection and coordinates the implementation and sustainment of protective measures to protect assets according to the commander's priorities. During the planning process, the protection cell provides input to the commander's MDMP by integrating the threat and hazard assessment with the commander's EEFI, CAL, and DAL. While the planning cell develops plans, the protection cell attempts to minimize vulnerability based on the developing COA. The intent is to identify and recommend refinements to the COA that are necessary to reduce vulnerability and ensure mission success. The protection cell provides vulnerability mitigation measures to help reduce risks associated with a particular COA and conducts planning and oversight for full spectrum operations. Representatives from the protection cell may provide input to plans and future operations, depending on the OE and the commander's preference. Commanders tailor and augment the protection cell with functional expertise to form a protection working group as the mission requires.

5-3. A chief of protection is assigned to the modular division, corps, and theater Army headquarters. At brigade and below, the commander normally designates a senior leader to this role. The AMD coordinator, engineer coordinator, provost marshal, or CBRN officer may be designated as a protection coordinator to support integration. Chiefs of protection and protection coordinators participate in various forums to facilitate the continuous integration of protection tasks and systems in the operations process. This typically occurs through protection working groups in a theater of operations and in force protection working groups and executive forums as part of the installation force protection program.

5-4. The protection working group is led by the chief of protection and normally consists of—

- AMD officer.
- AT officer.
- CBRN officer.
- Engineer officer.
- EOD officer.
- OPSEC officer.
- Provost marshal.
- Intelligence representative.
- PR officer.
- G-6 representative.
- Public affairs officer.
- Staff judge advocate.

Note. Depending on the OE or type of operation, the commander may add G-7; assistant chief of staff, civil affairs operations (G-9); surgeon; and safety; information engagement; medical; and CA staff officers.

5-5. At the division level, subordinate units normally provide a liaison officer to the working group meetings. The protection cells in division, corps, and Army headquarters integrate protection functions into the operations process.

5-6. The protection working group—

- Helps the commander establish protection priorities by developing the CAL and DAL.
- Provides a forum for evaluating assumptions made in protection planning and for recommending adjustments to protection efforts.
- May help deconflict protection responsibilities, recommend C2 relationships necessary for specific protection efforts, facilitate adjacent unit coordination, or allocate protection resources.
- Considers various time horizons from the current organizational battle rhythm through future operations.

5-7. While there are subtle differences, each is organized along similar lines and can perform similar functions. The division and corps differ in that the corps is more likely to be a joint or multinational headquarters, and it often has a larger AO. All protection cells, especially at the theater level, have unique characteristics with different organizations, coordinators, sections, and abilities, depending on the mission they are conducting.

5-8. The protection cell helps develop a concept of protection tailored to the type of operation the unit is conducting. Figure 5-1 shows an MEB supporting a division with three BCTs and one aviation brigade. A mission analysis for the operation determined requirements that could be best satisfied by one or more MEBs. Based on the mission variables, the protection working group in the division main command post recommended the mix of capabilities needed for the MEB. Here, the MEB is focused on completing specific protection tasks and providing support to maneuver units. The MEB typically adjusts command and support relationships accordingly. The protection cell may make recommendations to the division on the task organization of protection assets or the type of C2 relationship needed to reduce high risks. This example depicts the employment of an MEB for protection tasks; however, in operations without an MEB, the protection cell may recommend protection strategies from reinforcing and complementary capabilities found in other formations for use in primary and economy-of-force roles.

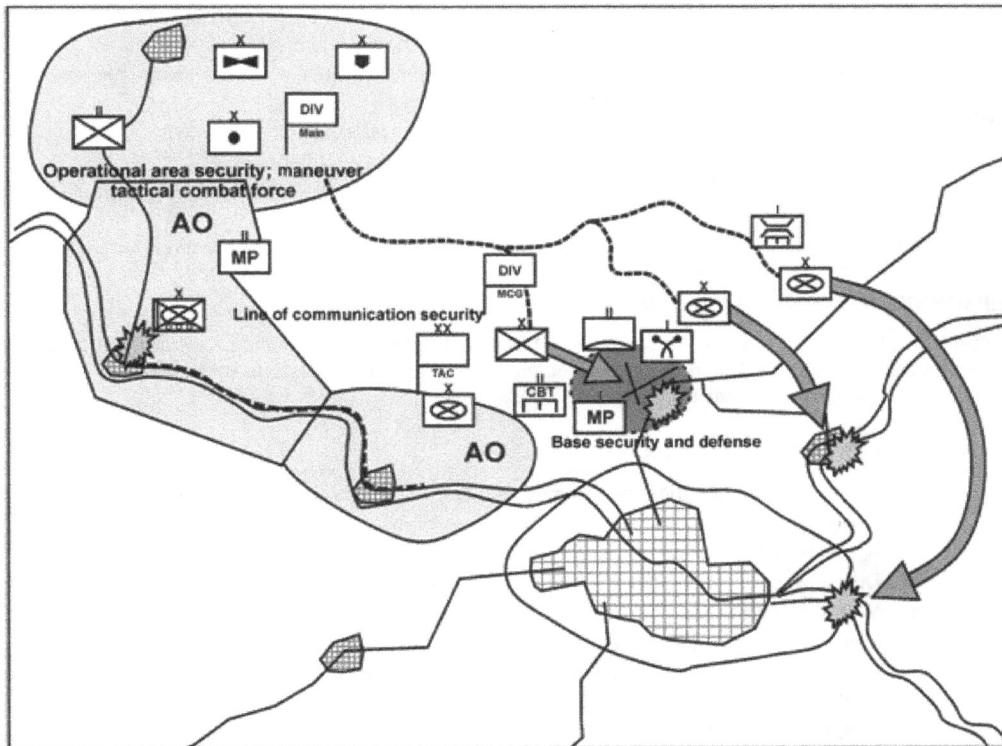

Figure 5-1. Sample protection concept for offensive operations

COMPOSITION

5-9. The protection cell membership does not require representatives from every functional element of protection. However, these members provide a dedicated staff that is able to coordinate with other appropriate coordinating, personal, and special staff elements. Primary members of the protection cell typically include the chief of protection, AMD officer, PR officer, OPSEC officer, provost marshal, CBRN officer, EOD officer, engineer officer, and AT officer.

CHIEF OF PROTECTION

5-10. The chief of protection may be designated by tables of organization and equipment or by the unit commander. He is the principal advisor to the commander on all matters relating to the protection warfighting function. A chief of protection—

- Plans and coordinates protection functions and missions.
- Advises the commander on where to allocate and employ protection capabilities.
- Chairs protection working group meetings, coordinates input, and makes recommendations to the commander regarding CALs and DALs.
- Manages the writing of the protection annex and provides input to plans, orders, branches, and sequels.
- Synchronizes with other staff cells, nodes, and functional groups.
- Provides guidance on the execution of protection tasks and systems.
- Continually monitors and assesses the overall protection effort.

AIR AND MISSILE DEFENSE OFFICER

5-11. The AMD officer coordinates and synchronizes the AMD tasks in the AO. He—

- Advises, monitors, and makes recommendations regarding the current enemy air and missile threat.
- Collaborates with higher headquarters to protect critical and defended assets.
- Coordinates current operations of subordinate air defense artillery forces.
- Coordinates adjustments of sensor and engagement coverage based on changes in the mission variables.
- Leads or augments other protection components when operating in a low-threat air environment.

PERSONNEL RECOVERY OFFICER

5-12. The PR officer advises the commander on all aspects of PR operations. He plans and coordinates operations necessary to obtain the release or recovery of captured, missing, or isolated personnel from uncertain or hostile environments and denied areas.

OPERATIONS SECURITY OFFICER

5-13. The OPSEC officer identifies and recommends critical information requirements. He—

- Analyzes adversaries and vulnerabilities as part of the IPB process.
- Assesses OPSEC risk.
- Develops, coordinates, and applies OPSEC measures across the staff.
- Writes the OPSEC estimate and tab to the protection appendix.
- Monitors, assesses, and adjusts OPSEC measures in terms of their MOE and MOP.
- Reviews internal staff documents, information system logs, and news releases for sensitive information and compromised EEFI.
- Searches news sources, weblogs, and other Web sites for sensitive information and compromised EEFI.

PROVOST MARSHAL

5-14. The provost marshal plans military police support for operations and provides advice on military police capabilities. He—

- Makes recommendations on developing and allocating military police resources that protect CALs and DALs.
- Synchronizes military police operations and law enforcement guidance between main and tactical command posts and among subordinate, adjacent, and higher units.
- Provides military police and physical security planning expertise, including—
  - Area security.
  - Police engagement.
  - Internment/resettlement and detainee operations.
  - Area damage control.
  - Consequence management operations.
  - Base defense operations.
  - Response force operations.
  - Critical site and asset security.
  - C2 node protection.
  - Straggler and displaced-civilian control.
  - Law enforcement.
  - Criminal investigations.

- U.S. customs operations.
- Host nation police development and transition operations.
- AT operations.
- Police intelligence operations.
- Makes recommendations on assigning protective service details to HRP. These protective service details may be organic unit assets or an adjacent or higher unit passing through the division AO.
- May serve as a member of a vulnerability assessment team.
- Coordinates with the engineer officer to plan support and protection of river-crossing operations and main supply route security and protection.

CHEMICAL, BIOLOGICAL, RADIOLOGICAL, AND NUCLEAR OFFICER

5-15. The CBRN officer conducts planning for and oversees all CBRN operations. He—

- Provides response analysis, written estimates and plans, and advice.
- Provides staff supervision for CBRN site assessments and consequence management operations in the AO.
- Plans CBRN support with higher and adjacent units.
- Supports the CBRN warning and reporting system.
- Recommends how to employ CBRN assets.
- Coordinates with the engineer officer for explosive hazard operations by identifying the appropriate mix of complementary and reinforcing capabilities.

EXPLOSIVE ORDNANCE DISPOSAL OFFICER

5-16. The EOD officer incorporates EOD requirements into plans and orders. He—

- Recommends how to implement EOD-unique skills.
- Tracks UXO, IED, and WMD incident support.
- Recommends reinforcing support.

5-17. If assigned to the headquarters, the explosive hazards coordination cell can assist the protection cell through the collection, analysis, and dissemination of explosive hazard information. This cell is a specialized Army engineer force pool unit assigned to corps, division, or brigade staffs. Within the theater, it can predict, track, distribute information on, and mitigate explosive hazards that affect force application, focused logistics, survivability, and situational awareness.

ENGINEER OFFICER

5-18. The engineer officer identifies requirements and prioritizes engineer capabilities and assets. He—

- Identifies current and future operations that require force packaging to meet operational requirements.
- Identifies and synchronizes requirements for the mobility of friendly forces.
- Identifies requirements for safeguarding bases.
- Advises on the aspects of survivability as defined in chapter 2.
- Facilitates the sustainment of friendly forces.
- Identifies general engineering operations.
- Synchronizes with the CBRN officer to apply battlefield obscuration and decontamination support as appropriate.
- Provides reachback to the Army Corps of Engineers.
- Contributes to a clear understanding of the physical environment.
- Provides support to noncombatants, other nations, and civilian authorities and agencies.

ANTITERRORISM OFFICER

5-19. The AT officer—

- Establishes an AT program.
- Collects, analyzes, and disseminates threat information.
- Assesses and reduces critical vulnerabilities (conducts AT assessments).
- Increases AT awareness in Soldiers, civilians, and family members.
- Maintains defense according to the FPCON.
- Establishes civil/military partnerships for terrorist incident crises.
- Conducts terrorism threat/incident response planning.
- Conducts exercises and evaluates/assesses AT plans.

PROTECTION IN BRIGADES AND BELOW

5-20. Commanders at brigade and below echelons are not organized with dedicated protection staff cells, but they are still responsible for integrating the protection warfighting function into full spectrum operations. Protection integration at these echelons may require commanders to designate a staff lead (protection officer) who has the experience to integrate risk management and other integrating processes. These duties could be accomplished by the deputy brigade commander, executive officer, operations officer, or a sergeant major. Assistant operations officers and other staff members could be designated as protection coordinators to facilitate the integration of the twelve protection tasks and systems into operations. In all cases, protection officers and coordinators work with higher and lower echelons to nest protection activities with complementary and reinforcing capabilities.

DIVISION PROTECTION CELL

5-21. The protection cell in the main command post consists of seven staff groups, including the chief of protection. The staff members focus their particular areas of expertise and on the integration and synchronization of division protection efforts. The protection cell informs the commander of changes or threats to CALs and DALs.

5-22. The tactical command post contains a small protection cell that consists of provost marshal, AMD, and CBRNE sections. It plans, coordinates, and synchronizes protection and functional capabilities for units under the tactical command post C2. Staff members in the main command post provide other critical protection information to the tactical command post organization as required. These members work throughout the coordinating and support staff and in designated cells. The two groups work closely together to integrate and synchronize the protection effort across the AO (internally and externally) with joint, interagency, and multinational assets.

CORPS PROTECTION CELL

5-23. The protection cell at the corps level is similar in organization and purpose to the division protection cell. It is comprised of CBRN, EOD, engineer, military police, and AMD personnel and is typically led by the chief of protection. This cell serves to coordinate, synchronize, and integrate complementary and reinforcing capabilities supporting the corps headquarters to provide protection throughout corps subordinate units and in the corps AO. The corps protection cell integrates and monitors OPSEC actions at all levels, while managing the effects of CBRNE, physical and area security, survivability, and air and missile threats to corps operations. The corps protection cell is typically augmented for stability operations and may serve as the center of consequence management efforts to manage and mitigate problems resulting from natural and man-made disasters or terrorist incidents.

ARMY SERVICE COMPONENT COMMAND PROTECTION CELL

5-24. Theater command posts have a dedicated protection element instrumental for reachback. *Reachback* is the process of obtaining products, services, and applications, or forces, or equipment, or material from organizations that are not forward deployed. (JP 3-30) Theater command posts can exploit resources, capabilities, and expertise while physically located outside the theater or in a joint operations area. They also coordinate unified actions and oversee protection for the theater within the combatant commander's area of responsibility.

5-25. Figure 5-2 shows the operational protection directorate at the theater level, which is where corps or other task-organized units normally receive protection guidance from higher headquarters. Similar to the cells at corps and division, the operational protection directorate requires expertise from other staff sections to synthesize the information required to oversee the entire protection function.

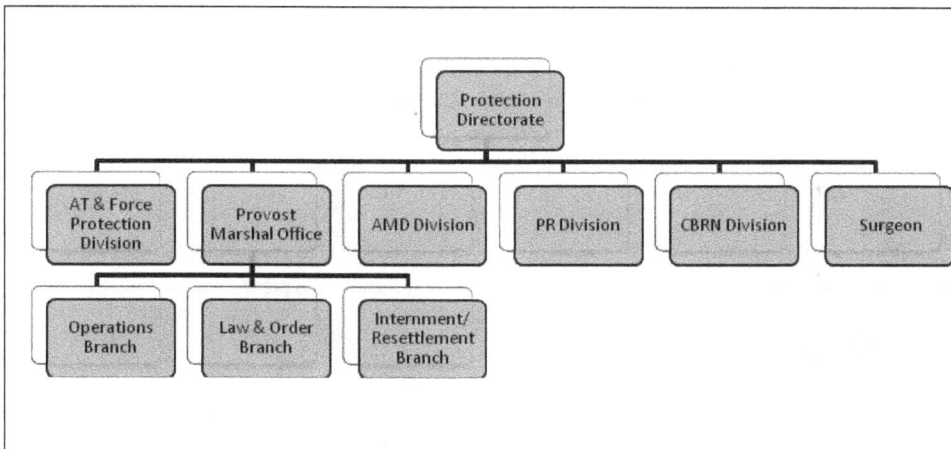

Figure 5-2. Sample protection directorate at theater level

5-26. The theater is the first level of command with a dedicated AT and protection division that adds an in-theater source of staff support for subordinates. This command is also the first level with a dedicated surgeon cell to conduct casualty prevention planning. Protection cells at division and corps require assistance from these elements when planning casualty prevention measures. The early-entry command post protection cell is tailored to the needs of the mission at hand but has full reachback to main and operational command posts. Protecting information in the theater is not the responsibility of the operational protection directorate; the theater G-6 and G-7 share responsibility for information protection.

5-27. With the exception of U.S. Army North, the theater typically resources the protection warfighting function to support Army forces in theater and joint and allied forces. Often, the theater may be designated as the joint security coordinator and be responsible for the joint security area. (See JP 3-10 for more information.) The theater protection cell (with augmented joint, interagency, and multinational forces) provides the nucleus of the joint security coordination center. The theater may designate an MEB to serve as its operational protection headquarters, receiving mission orders to supervise selected forces (including TCFs). Rear operations centers (area) may provide specified base C2 and security management for critical bases and facilities.

PROTECTION WORKING GROUP

5-28. OCONUS, the theater typically resources the protection warfighting function to support Army forces in theater and joint and allied forces. Consequently, Army service component commands have several theater level commands and brigades that contribute force in support of the protection function.

5-29. The protection cell forms the core membership of the protection working group and includes other agencies as required. Protection cell and protection working group members differ, in that additional staff officers are brought into the working group. These additional officers meet operational requirements for threat assessments, vulnerability assessments, and protection priority recommendations. The protection working group does not merit additional manpower, but calls upon existing resources across the staff.

5-30. Commanders incorporate daily, weekly, or monthly protection working group meetings into the unit battle rhythm as needed. The meetings have the same purpose, regardless of the echelon. Protection functions at different echelons of command differ mostly in the size of the AO and the number of available protection capabilities. The protection working group—

- Determines likely threats and hazards from updated enemy tactics, the environment, and accidents.
- Determines vulnerabilities as assessed by the vulnerability assessment team.
- Establishes and recommends protection priorities, such as the CAL.
- Provides recommendations for the CAL and DAL.
- Reviews and coordinates unit protection measures.
- Recommends FPCONs and random AT measures.
- Determines required resources and makes recommendations for funding and equipment fielding.
- Provides input and recommendations on protection-related training.
- Makes recommendations to commanders on protection issues that require a decision.
- Performs tasks required for a force protection working group and a threat protection working group according to Department of Defense Instruction (DODI) 2000.16.
- Accesses assets and infrastructure that are designated as critical by higher headquarters.

5-31. Table 5-1 shows a sample purpose, agenda, and composition of a protection working group with staff inputs and outputs, and Table 5-2 shows a sample protection working group created for vulnerability assessments.

Table 5-1. Sample protection working group activities

PURPOSE	AGENDA	
The protection working group monitors and assesses the risks and threats to forces in the AO and implements control measures to maintain the protection by— • Reviewing threats and hazards. • Identifying vulnerabilities. • Recommending countermeasures, FPCON levels, assessments, missions, and tasks to components. • Monitoring corrective actions. • Directing vulnerability assessment teams.	• Operations/intelligence update. • CCIR/concept of operation review. • DAL update. • New vulnerabilities (next 72 hours). • Extremely high/high-risk mitigation measures. • Recommendations (security posture adjustments, troop behavior, command information engagement, resource allocation, required training). • Conclusion.	
COMPOSITION	INPUT	OUTPUT
• Chief of protection (chair). • G-2. • Major subordinate command and FOB AT officers. • Staff judge advocate. • EOD officer. • Engineer officer. • Provost marshal. • Surgeon. • Safety officer. • CBRN officer. • OPSEC officer. • Others, as required.	• Commander's guidance and intent. • Current and emerging threats and trends. • Current operations update. • Major subordinate command/FOB vulnerability assessments. • Vulnerability assessment team assessments and trends.	• Updated protection assessment. • Identified vulnerabilities. • Recommended FPCON. • Recommended mitigation TTP and tasks. • Recommended changes to EEFI. • Recommended changes to the CAL and DAL.

Table 5-2. Sample protection working group for vulnerability assessment

MISSION	ASSESSMENT OUTLINE
The protection working group works with the higher headquarters vulnerability assessment team. It evaluates implemented protection measures and identifies existing vulnerabilities at specified sites and all locations, facilities, and bases used by contractors and coalition personnel. The end result is that the protection working group provides a safe, secure environment in which friendly forces can live and perform their duties by— • Identifying and assessing threats and vulnerabilities. • Recommending countermeasures. • Reporting through the chief of protection to the commander.	• AT/force protection plan review (all). • Local threat assessment (G-2). • Physical security (provost marshal). • Entry control point procedures (provost marshal). • Perimeter defense (protection noncommissioned officer). • Base defense operations center (chief of protection). • High-density facilities (protection noncommissioned officer). • Emergency medical response (surgeon). • Structural and facility force protection standards (engineer officer). • CBRN defense (protection noncommissioned officer). • HRP (provost marshal).
COMPOSITION	REFERENCES/STANDARDS
• Chief of protection. • Protection noncommissioned officer. • OPSEC officer. • G-2. • Engineer officer. • Provost marshal. • Surgeon. • Safety officer. • G-7.	• OPORDs. • Protection Plans. • GTA 90-01-010, JCOB Force Protection Handbook. • DOD O-2000.12-H. • DODI 2000.16. • UFC 4-010-01. • UFC 4-010-02.

This page intentionally left blank.

Appendix A

Protection in Force Projection Operations

Army forces need strategic and operational reach to deploy and immediately conduct operations with little or no advanced notice anywhere in the world. Expeditionary operations require units that can deploy and conduct extended operations. Units depend on joint-enabled force projection and protection for deployment, sustainment, and protection across intercontinental distances in full spectrum operations. Units available and ready to deploy begin the force projection process upon receiving a warning order or deployment order. Army and joint operations require successful onward movement, protected personnel, and accompanied materiel. Continuing protection measures must be taken from home station, to reception in theater, and to integration into the AO. In each phase, deploying and supported commanders apply elements of the protection warfighting function based on the analysis and recommendations of their respective protection cells.

PLANNING AND PREPARATION DURING PREDEPLOYMENT ACTIVITIES

A-1. During the movement from home station to the deployment location, unit personnel and equipment may arrive at different ports of debarkation. Protection during movement can be difficult as units pass through various areas of responsibility. The Army uses five steps in planning and preparation during predeployment activities. During deployment, commanders apply protection measures in each step to protect the force.

- *Step 1.* Analyze the mission.
- *Step 2.* Structure the forces.
- *Step 3.* Refine the deployment data.
- *Step 4.* Prepare the force.
- *Step 5.* Schedule movement.

Note. See FMI 3-35 for more information.

ANALYZE THE MISSION

A-2. Commanders examine the mission and develop COAs, using employment considerations as the primary planning factor. A primary protection consideration depends on the type of entry operation conducted. Forced-entry operations require extensive mission analysis to adequately protect the force. Deployment into a permissive environment requires forces to assess the host nation security, police forces, and port security operations. Planners do not assume that existing or host nation units at the site will automatically provide protection. All deployed U.S. units arrive prepared to protect themselves based on the threat at the site location.

STRUCTURE THE FORCE

A-3. While developing COAs, planners identify forces based on their capabilities to accomplish specific missions. Commanders establish protection measures and force requirements based on the threat assessment of theater ports and intermediate staging bases. Intelligence and threat information is critical in determining the force structure. Commanders factor protection requirements into time-phased, force and deployment data planning. Experiences from worldwide deployments, especially those in Operations Iraqi Freedom and Enduring Freedom, demonstrate how early protection planning and the execution of protective measures can substantially reduce the risk to deploying forces.

REFINE THE DEPLOYMENT DATA

A-4. As planners identify forces, they begin developing time-phased, force and deployment data. The supported combatant commander defines the intent for deployment. The commander's intent may be specific and direct the sequence of units or simply identify a general deployment timeline. Protection considerations often determine the first deployers for protection-related missions and tasks in the joint operations area. Commanders compare the situation in the joint operations area against available lift assets to determine the appropriate deployment sequence. Host nation restrictions and sensitivities may limit protection options, creating a need for close coordination with assets already in the joint operations area. While protecting the initial-entry force, commanders balance the need for rapid response with the mix of combat power and resources that accomplish the mission. This balance provides protection, efficient deployment, and a range of options for responding to possible conditions.

PREPARE THE FORCE

A-5. Planners develop force packages to ensure that the right capabilities, in the proper combinations, support the combatant commander. Protection considerations include determining the casualty prevention measures required to protect the force against health risks. Before deploying, units conduct risk assessments to determine their vulnerabilities. These assessments provide a baseline from which to implement appropriate protection measures that reduce or mitigate risk.

SCHEDULE MOVEMENT

A-6. Correctly sequencing forces to deploy provides the commander with capabilities to achieve the desired objectives. Once commanders put a strategic lift schedule into motion, it is difficult to change without losing the transportation capacity. Protection considerations consist of front-loading appropriate units to provide protection and security. The units draw equipment first and then support follow-on units with staging and onward movement. These units should arrive in theater early in the deployment process to provide better protection and movement security. Protection and security are essential to promptly move combat forces forward.

A-7. Commanders also implement another protection consideration—proactive OPSEC measures. These measures limit public knowledge of in-transit force movements, including U.S. military ship and aircraft flights and intratheater movements of key personnel, equipment, and logistics.

A-8. A final protection consideration includes reviewing and, if necessary, modifying contracting processes and transportation agreements. This consideration meets DOD protection and AT standards.

DEPLOYMENT

A-9. Table A-1 lists theater and deploying division or corps protection cell requirements for the synchronization and execution of protection measures during deployment.

A-10. During the force projection process, four distinct and interrelated deployment phases occur. These phases may not be sequential; they can overlap or occur simultaneously.

- Predeployment activities.
- Movement to and activities at the port of embarkation.
- Movement to the port of debarkation.
- Reception, staging, onward movement, and integration (RSO&I).

Table A-1. Protection synchronization for deployment

Protection Tasks and Systems	Predeployment Activities	Movement to Port of Embarkation	Movement to Port of Debarkation	RSO&I
AMD	• Perform AMD threat assessment. • Prepare force packages.	• Coordinate transportation protective measures for sensitive arms, ammunition, and explosives.	• Maintain transportation protective measures for sensitive arms, ammunition, and explosives.	• Coordinate advance deployment of force packages.
PR	• Complete DD Form 1833 (Isolated Personnel Report). • Establish PR organization. • Cross-staff coordination. • Analyze PR gap. • Integrate diplomatic/ military/civil PR. • Establish PR SOPs. • Exercise/rehearse.	• Establish PR organization. • Cross-staff coordination. • Analyze PR gap. • Integrate diplomatic/ military/civil PR. • Review PR SOPs. • Exercise/rehearse • Coordinate PR support while in transit.	• Establish PR organization. • Cross-staff coordination. • Analyze PR gap. • Integrate diplomatic/ military/civil PR. • Exercise PR SOPs. • Exercise/rehearse. • Coordinate PR support while in transit.	• Transfer unit isolated personnel report data to theater staff. • Establish PR organization. • Cross-staff coordination. • Analyze PR gap. • Integrate diplomatic/ military/civil PR. • Exercise PR SOPs. • Exercise/rehearse. • Coordinate PR support while building combat power.
Information protection	• Deconflict host nation frequency, taboo frequencies (911), friendly radars, or jammers. • Ensure uninterrupted access to joint distributed planning (virtual collaboration) and training amongst geographically dispersed units. • Gain theater network configuration and resource allocation to DISN services or SATCOM.	• Prestage critical BCCS data at OCONUS area processing centers. • Support en route mission planning and updating of critical information (orders, overlays, intelligence).	• Ensure immediate satellite access to retrieve current battle command data updated during communications blackout. • Deploy liaison officers to OCONUS area processing centers to ensure or coordinate access to unit prestaged data.	• Assist in coordinating business continuity and disaster recovery solutions. • Assist in updating risk analysis. • Assist in meeting legal and regulatory compliance. • Assist in coordinating physical (environmental) security.
Fratricide avoidance	• Train on combat identification processes and procedures.	• Maintain situational awareness.	• Maintain situational awareness.	• Review fratricide prevention procedures with Soldiers and check equipment.
Operational area security	• Plan for adequate protection during RSO&I. • Plan for proper sequencing of forces to ensure adequate combat power. • Establish CAL.	• Coordinate and assess port security transportation protective services. • Coordinate movement with local police.	• Assign supercargoes. • Store cargo and measures in place. • Ensure that the Army Criminal Investigation Command conducts logistics security operations.	• Ensure that adequate security forces are available to protect the force during RSO&I and movement to tactical assembly areas.
AT	• Provide Level I AT training. • Complete threat assessment. • Complete criticality assessment. • Complete vulnerability assessment. • Form installation force protection working group.	• Coordinate interagency security measures. • Submit AT plan to combatant commander. • Assemble port readiness committees. • Develop HRP security measures.	• Track all units during transit. • Employ countersurveillance and counterintelligence resources.	• Conduct port vulnerability assessments. • Brief unit on threat levels. • Brief unit on ROE. • Implement planned security measures.
Survivability	• Assess Soldier, equipment, and vehicle protective requirements.	• Conduct survivability.	• Conduct survivability.	• Conduct necessary survivability support.

Table A-1. Protection synchronization for deployment (continued)

Protection Tasks and Systems	Predeployment Activities	Movement to Port of Embarkation	Movement to Port of Debarkation	RSO&I
FHP	• Coordinate for individual medical readiness processing programs. • Survey the AO to determine health threats. • Plan and coordinate for preventive medicine support requirements. • Perform food and water vulnerability assessments. • Plan and coordinate for veterinary services. • Develop procedures to inspect, monitor, and submit food and water samples. • Plan for animal disease prevention and control program. • Develop a plan to meet or improve the stress control needs of Soldiers and units. • Inform Soldiers about good oral hygiene and preventive dentistry measures. • Plan and coordinate area medical laboratory deployment.	• Conduct continual assessment.	• Conduct continual assessment.	• Continue to execute the mission plan, adjusting to protect Soldiers from potential health threats.
CBRN operations	• Complete CBRN threat assessment and enemy capability evaluation. • Complete friendly forces unit status evaluation. • Develop CBRN defense plan.	• Maintain situational awareness.	• Maintain situational awareness.	• Review AT plan with combatant commander (command authority).
Safety	• Train and license Soldiers in handling hazmat. • Conduct safety oversight. • Conduct safety awareness briefings.	• Provide quality assurance specialist ammunition surveillance support. • Train load team to standards. • Review accident/near-miss data to develop loss reduction plans.	• Provide troop rest and hydration. • Review accident/near-miss data to develop loss reduction plans.	• Acclimatize troops. • Train with night vision. • Enforce safe vehicle operations. • Train rollover and recovery operations. • Conduct safety oversight. • Conduct safety awareness briefings. • Review accident/near-miss data to develop loss reduction plans.
OPSEC	• Recommend CCIR. • Conduct OPSEC vulnerability assessment. • Conduct OPSEC training. • Incorporate OPSEC into planning activities.	• Conduct OPSEC.	• Conduct OPSEC.	• Conduct OPSEC.
EOD	• Provide EOD threat assessment and enemy evaluation. • Provide IED awareness training. • Ensure equipment readiness.	• Maintain situational awareness.	• Maintain situational awareness.	• Review current enemy procedures for future AO or movement to tactical assembly areas. • Provide theater-specific training.

PREDEPLOYMENT ACTIVITIES

A-11. During predeployment activities through the fort-to-port phase, the U.S. Army Installation Management Command is a critical protection and force projection enabler. This command manages most Army installations worldwide. Its garrison commanders play a critical role in successfully protecting deploying forces as they execute force projection operations in CONUS. Installation provost marshals (with military police) protect assets as the unit prepares to deploy. Safety, medical, and information management personnel protect personnel and information. Division and corps protection cells coordinate closely with the installation and garrison staff to identify which information and assets to protect and to apply appropriate protection and security measures that are consistent with the threat analysis.

A-12. At Army installations, AT working groups work as forums to involve installation protection personnel with federal, state, and local law enforcement officials. Together, they identify potential threats to the installation and improve interagency communications. Before deployment, division and corps protection cells coordinate with the installation staff to develop protective measures as required by the local threat assessments. In addition, coordination may be required with port security personnel and the combatant commander for protection requirements in the AO.

A-13. OPSEC and information protection are also key protection tasks during predeployment activities. Effective OPSEC keeps adversaries from exploiting friendly deployment and staging information. Commanders also ensure that their rear detachment commanders and family readiness groups take appropriate OPSEC measures.

A-14. Commanders consider the AT element of protection during predeployment activities. Each deploying unit (battalion or larger) should have at least one assigned Level II AT officer. This individual must have completed a service-sponsored certification course. The deploying unit commander (assisted by the AT officer) ensures that AT plans are integrated into movements through high-threat areas. Before deployment, units assess risk by conducting threat, criticality, and vulnerability assessments. Units conduct the assessments far enough in advance of deployment to allow for the development of necessary protection measures for deploying assets.

A-15. After the notification, commanders at all levels begin to issue planning guidance as they plan, prepare, execute, and assess the deployment order. Unit commanders analyze the protection requirements and determine which resources adequately protect the deploying force. Finding the proper balance between protecting the force and rapidly projecting the force is critical. Commanders seek an appropriate balance of protection, rapid deployment, and adequate support.

A-16. Before arriving in an area of responsibility, commanders submit protection plans through their higher headquarters to the geographic combatant commander (this does not apply to the units deploying to the USNORTHCOM area of responsibility). The protection measures in the deploying unit plan must match the guidance developed by the geographic combatant commander, who coordinates and approves individual plans.

MOVEMENT TO AND ACTIVITIES AT THE PORT OF EMBARKATION

A-17. During some phases of deployment, DOD transfers custody of its military equipment to non-DOD entities, including foreign-owned ships crewed by non-U.S. citizens. The protection cell ensures that contract processes for transportation movements meet DOD security requirements. Figure A-1, page A-6, shows various deployment activities and the agencies responsible for them.

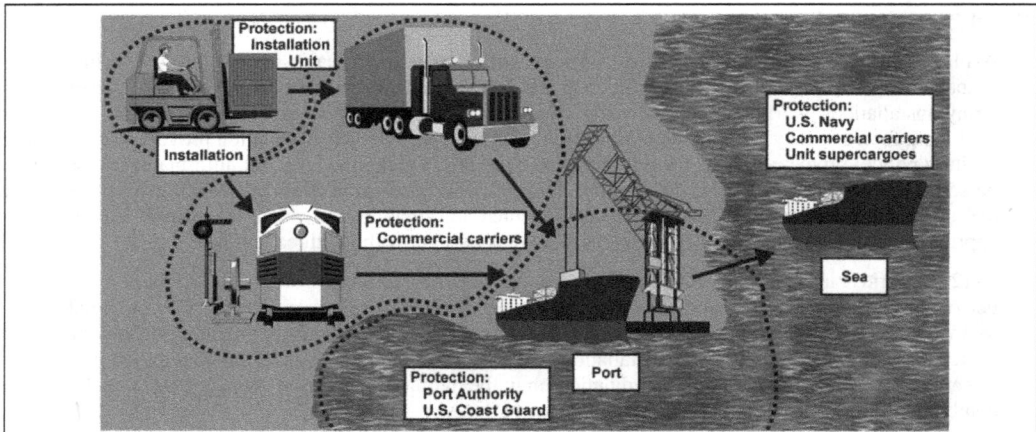

	Load Material	Protection	Transport by Land	Protection	Stage Cargo and Load Vessel	Protection	Transport by Sea	Protection
Activity								
Responsibility	Installation	Installation: DA police Military police	Commercial rail and moving carriers	Commercial carriers	Port readiness committee	Port authority U.S. Coast Guard	U.S. Navy	U.S. Navy
	Commander	Unit guards	Surface Deployment and Distribution Command	Local law enforcement	Unit	Supercargoes	Commercial carriers	Commercial carriers
	Unit	Supercargoes	Unit	Supercargoes	NA	NA	Maritime administration	Unit supercargoes

Note. The protection cell must assess the assets and carriers and, in coordination with the Surface Deployment and Distribution Command, provide additional protection measures consistent with threat and sensitive-cargo requirements.

Figure A-1. Protection responsibilities during deployment

A-18. Deploying units traditionally focus protection efforts on their impending overseas operations. However, the protection cell staff must frequently coordinate with CONUS-based agencies. Protection responsibilities for Army units deploying through commercial seaports are divided among joint and interagency organizations. These organizations include the U.S. Army Materiel Command (Surface Deployment Distribution Command, Army Contracting Command, and Army Sustainment Command), U.S. Transportation Command, Military Sealift Command, USNORTHCOM, and U.S. Army Forces Command. Because the protection tasks that the Army may conduct outside its installations are limited, the protection staff works closely with federal, state, and local agencies. Together, they ensure that adequate protection measures exist and that they are executed during deployments through strategic seaports.

A-19. Although transportation organizations and activities may provide limited organic protection, the deploying unit commander plans protection measures for rail and highway movements. The protection cell, in coordination with the Surface Deployment and Distribution Command, continually assesses the assets and carriers. It also provides additional protection measures consistent with the threat and sensitive-cargo requirements. These measures may include the use of contract security personnel or unit guards to protect unit assets, but the commander makes the final determination based on security requirements. The protection cell coordinates with the installation transportation officer (CONUS) or movement control team (OCONUS) and authorized railroad or commercial truck carriers on guard and escort matters.

A-20. The protection cell coordinates with the port readiness committee at each strategic port. These committees provide deploying unit commanders with common coordination structures for DOD; the U.S. Coast Guard; and other federal, state, and local agencies at the port level. When military equipment is being moved, the committees act as principal interfaces between DOD and other officials at ports.

A-21. In coordination with other DOD activities and port authorities, the U.S. Transportation Command and Surface Deployment and Distribution Command administer the DOD transportation security program. This program provides standardized transportation security measures, constant oversight, and central direction. In CONUS, commanders plan protection measures for units and equipment en route to the port, while the Surface Deployment and Distribution Command coordinates security at the port.

A-22. Depending on the threat assessment, units may guard equipment while at the installation, at railheads, or en route to ports of embarkation. Units may consider assigning supercargoes to accompany the equipment during transit from the seaport of embarkation to the seaport of debarkation.

A-23. DOD 4500.9-R specifies governing requirements for moving sensitive military cargo. It establishes various levels of required protection and monitoring based on risk categories. Protection and monitoring measures range from simple seals used in shipping to continuous cargo surveillance. The regulation establishes protection requirements for cargo and outlines the transportation protective services available to meet them. The cargo sensitivity and means of transportation determine how the Surface Deployment and Distribution Command protects military cargo. Table A-2 provides examples of transportation protective services required for various types of sensitive items and equipment.

Note. See DOD Regulation 4500.9-R, part II, chapter 205 for more information.

Table A-2. Examples of transportation protective services

Security Risk Code	Risk Category	Example	Minimum TPS
1	Highest risk AA&E CAT I	Man-portable missiles	PSS/SNS/EXC SEV
2	Medium-high risk CAT II	Automatic weapons, landmines	PSS/SNS/EXC[1] SEV if FPCON Charlie
	Medium risk CAT II	High-explosive grenades[2]	PSS/SNS/EXC[1] SEV if FPCON Charlie
3	Low risk CAT III and IV	Small arms, smoke grenades	DDP/SNS
4	Low risk CAT III and IV	Small arms, smoke grenades	DDP/SNS
5	CAT I	Weapons with secret guidance systems	PSS/SNS/EXC SEV
6	CAT I	Weapons with confidential guidance systems	PSS/SNS/EXC SEV
7	Uncategorized demolitions (Div 1.1, 1.2, and 1.3 AA&E)[3]	Retrograde AA&E, howitzer cannons and barrels	DDP/SNS
8	Confidential CAT II	Weapons with confidential guidance systems[2]	PSS/SNS/EXC[1] SEV if FPCON Charlie
U	Uncontrolled/unclassified (Div 1.1, 1.2, and 1.3 AA&E)[3]	Bombs, torpedoes	DDP/SNS
S	Secret	Documents/hardware	DDP/SNS[4]
C	Confidential	Documents/hardware	CIS[5]
P	Pilferable, uncontrolled/ unclassified	Communications, electronics, high-value items	CIS and security tarps required for open-bed trailers[5]

[1]SEV is required for all U.S. Army CAT II shipments when pickup or drop off is in FPCON Charlie locations; SEV is not required for U.S. Air Force, Marine Corps, or Navy CAT II shipments at FPCON Charlie. However, SEV is required for CAT II shipments for all Services in FPCON Delta locations.
[2]Examples are not all-inclusive.
[3]For AA&E shipments weighing 150 pounds or less and 15 or fewer items, small arms weapons (CAT II through IV) and M-16 rifles (excluding .50-caliber and above rifles) use CIS.
[4]SNS is optional.
[5]DDP replaces CIS when the mileage exceeds 150.

A-24. The U.S. Army Criminal Investigation Command supports force projection and protection operations by providing logistics security to prevent theft, misappropriation, and other criminal acts.

A-25. During major combat operations, the U.S. Coast Guard conducts operations in littoral regions. These regions include port security and safety, military environmental response, maritime interdiction, coastal sea operations, and protection in territorial waters of the United States and overseas. In addition to waterside physical security, Coast Guard duties include—

- Regulating the shipping, handling, and pier side storage of hazardous cargo.
- Interfacing with military authorities as the senior DOD port safety agent.
- Issuing hazardous-cargo permits.
- Supervising vessel fire prevention programs.

MOVEMENT TO THE PORT OF DEBARKATION

A-26. *Supercargoes* are personnel that accompany cargo on board a ship for the purpose of accomplishing en route maintenance and security. (JP 1-02). Supercargoes represent the deploying unit commander when moving unit equipment by ship. They perform liaison during cargo reception at the seaport of embarkation, shipload and discharge operations, and clearance at the seaport of debarkation. The deploying unit may be required to provide supercargoes to accompany cargo aboard ships. At a minimum, commanders protect equipment against theft and pilferage.

A-27. Unit commanders recommend the composition of supercargoes. They determine the amount and types of equipment loaded aboard the ship, the number of units with equipment on the ship, and the required physical security measures. However, the Military Sealift Command determines the actual number of supercargoes permitted onboard based on the berthing capacity of the ship. Offload preparation parties may deploy with the advance party to help unload the vessel.

A-28. The size of the supercargo teams dedicated to each ship coincides with the team role. Commanders ensure that enough members to guard and maintain equipment are onboard, enough resources are available onboard, and enough money is available to finance additional costs for equipping and maintaining the team during the voyage. To prevent unnecessary commitment of personnel and resources, commanders closely coordinate supercargo teams with the Surface Deployment and Distribution Command, commercial carriers, and port facilities.

RECEPTION, STAGING, ONWARD MOVEMENT, AND INTEGRATION

A-29. RSO&I is the process of force closure in the AO. It requires a logistics infrastructure provided by the host nation or deployed sustainment assets. *Force closure* is the point in time when a supported joint force commander determines that sufficient personnel and equipment resources are in the assigned operational area to carry out assigned tasks. (JP 3-35) Reception is the first and most critical step of RSO&I. It marks the end of the strategic leg of deployment and the beginning of the operational use of forces. RSO&I aims to build the combat power necessary to support the combatant commander's concept of operation. Protection for units undergoing RSO&I falls under the protection cell of the theater supporting the combatant commander.

A-30. Planners carefully consider the threat assessment in the OE of RSO&I operations. A threat assessment gives commanders details of potential threats that can disrupt or block operations. The assessment also provides the level of infrastructure transportation and protection assets available to assist with onward movement. Commanders use this information to develop CALs and DALs.

A-31. When developing CALs and DALs, protection planners consider how changes in the tactical situation can create an urgent need for newly arrived units. Some units may be tasked for immediate employment. Heavy-equipment transport, military police, engineers, fuel support, and other assets necessary to move or protect equipment and personnel may become critical to mission success.

A-32. In a permissive environment, the host nation may be able to provide services and facilities to support protection. These services can lessen the requirement for U.S. forces to provide equivalent capabilities, thereby reducing the U.S. logistics footprint.

A-33. RSO&I operations can provide enemies with numerous opportunities to inflict serious casualties. These operations can delay the buildup of combat power by exploiting the vulnerability of units in transit from the theater staging base to the theater assembly area.

A-34. Units undergoing RSO&I present enemies with high-value, high-payoff targets. Any damage or destruction could result in serious delays in force closure. The advance deployment of military police units or other forces designated for area security become extremely important targets.

This page intentionally left blank.

Appendix B

Combat Identification

Combat identification gives U.S. forces the ability to avoid fratricide and differentiate among friendly, enemy, neutral, and unknown personnel and objects. Obtaining accurate combat identification is a problem as old as combat itself. Combat always has been, and always will be, confusing, complex, and deadly. Combat identification has become increasingly difficult with the advent of modern weaponry and tactics, the introduction of rapid fire and non-line-of-sight systems, and the desire to minimize collateral damage. A combat identification fratricide research study found that surface-to-surface and air-to-surface mission areas encompassed more than 90 percent of fratricide incidents. Primarily, target identification error and the lack of situational awareness caused these incidents.

DETECTION PROCESS

B-1. *Combat identification* is the process of attaining an accurate characterization of detected objects in the OE sufficient to support an engagement decision. (JP 3-09) (See JP 3-0 for more information.) Units achieve combat identification by applying situational awareness and target identification capabilities and by adhering to doctrine, TTP, and approved ROE that directly support a Soldier's engagement decision against objects in an OE. Combat identification attempts to avoid fratricide and unnecessary collateral damage.

B-2. Proper identification provides an accurate characterization of potential targets to allow engagement decisions with high confidence. Combat identification is not hardware-dependent; its capability combines the following:

- **Situational awareness.** Situational awareness provides the immediate knowledge of operation conditions, constrained geographically and in time.
- **Target identification.** Target identification provides the accurate and timely characterization of detected personnel and objects as friendly, neutral, enemy, or unknown. It is time-sensitive and directly supports a Soldier's target engagement decision. Quick and accurate target identification involves training and technology to maximize correct identification. Target identification provides two methods to distinguish targets:
  - **Cooperative.** Cooperative target identification requires intentional collaboration by the target.
  - **Noncooperative.** Noncooperative target identification exploits physical characteristics of the object and requires no cooperative action or response by the target.
- **Doctrine.** Sound doctrine provides a source of common understanding and interoperability. This knowledge directly contributes to Soldier ability to distinguish between friend and foe.
- **TTP.** TTP for combat identification provides the ability to identify a target, engage it while maintaining awareness of unknown targets, and avoid fratricide. Inadequate TTP or failure to rehearse them can cause hesitation, fratricide, and unnecessary collateral damage.
- **ROE.** *ROE* are directives issued by competent military authority that delineate the circumstances and limitations under which U.S. forces will initiate and/or continue combat engagement with other forces encountered. (JP 1-02) Critical to ROE is the rapid, accurate identification of potential targets. ROE are standardized throughout the AO to comply with higher headquarters guidance. If too restrictive, ROE could reduce combat effectiveness and put the force at greater risk. However, if ROE are too lax, they can lead to unnecessary collateral damage and fratricide. The greater the Soldier's ability to discriminate among friendly, enemy, neutral, and unknown personnel and objects, the less restrictive ROE may become. The military

authority developing ROE should consider combat identification capabilities when defining engagement criteria. Figure B-1 compares nonrestrictive and restrictive ROE and shows how they relate to casualties caused by enemy or friendly fires.

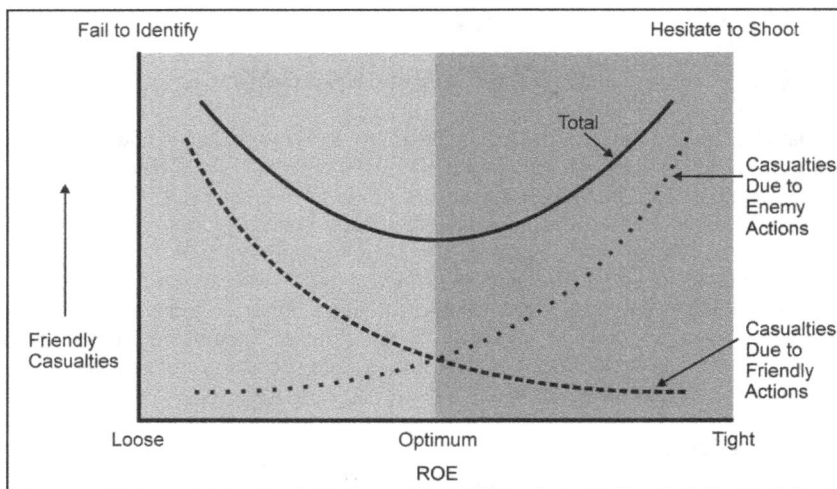

Figure B-1. Relationship between ROE and combat identification

LINKAGE

B-3. The range at which current weapons are effective exceeds the human ability to quickly and accurately identify all entities in the AO. Not only are Soldiers unable to fully exploit weapon advantages due to combat identification limitations, but these limitations also increase potential fratricide and unnecessary collateral damage. Enemies may use equipment with the same characteristics as those of friendly forces, or they may blend into the civilian populace during operations. To counter the enemy, U.S. forces can maneuver over larger areas, in more dispersed formations, and in contiguous and noncontiguous AOs. However, these abilities place more stress on existing fire control measures. When these factors combine with multinational operations (whose forces may have different or no combat identification aids or procedures), leaders must remain aware of how combat identification is functioning at all times.

B-4. Regardless of the combat identification, commanders need to interface technology with doctrine, TTP, and ROE. Combat identification standardizes the approach in deciding the appropriate level of force against all types of targets. It consists of—

- **Detection**—the discovery of any phenomena (personnel, equipment, objects) that are potential targets. Commanders can use detection from various means (visual observation, radar detection, electronic signals measurement).
- **Location**—the determination (by direction, reference point, or grid) of where a potential military target is located in the AO (ground or air).
- **Identification**—the determination of the friendly, hostile, unknown, or neutral character of a detected, potential target by its physical traits (size, shape, functional characteristics).
- **Classification**—the categorization of a potential target by the relative level of danger it represents.
- **Confirmation**—the rapid verification of a target in terms of the initial identification and classification. Soldiers and leaders confirm identification and classification of the target as an enemy before engaging. When engagement is considered, Soldiers answer the following questions:
  - Can I engage the target based on ROE?
  - What are the second- and third-order effects if I engage the target?

- Which target should I engage first (if there are multiple targets)?
- What is the best weapon system to use?

B-5. Planners and executors must remember that current cooperative target identification technology does not identify friend or foe—it only identifies friendly or unknown. Soldiers must decide whether to engage the target. Cooperative target identification is a tool for a final check before engagement; Soldiers should never use it as the sole criterion for target engagement.

B-6. Combat identification capability can be enhanced before detecting a potential target. It starts before operations, with planned fire and maneuver controls that minimize potential fratricide. Maintaining an accurate common operational picture provides continuously updated situational awareness to commanders and units, allowing leaders to control fires more effectively. Consequently, when Soldiers engage a target, they increase the likelihood of engaging correct targets with fewer or no negative, second- or third-order effects. These factors apply with surface-to-surface, air-to-surface, and surface-to-air engagements.

SURFACE TO SURFACE

B-7. The U.S. Army and Marine Corps developed combat identification capabilities to improve combat identification. Those capabilities are partitioned into the categories of information management tools, active and passive marking tools, and training tools:

- **Information management tools.** This category provides automatic locations of friendly forces, reported enemy sightings, obstacles, and known battlefield hazards. It provides satellite communications links to key leaders and critical platforms. There is a man-portable component that provides one-way, location data to the common operational picture. The system is typically composed of software and a hardware device.
- **Active marking tools.** Active marking tools include near-infrared programmable emitters for vehicles and flashing beacons for dismounted troops; second- and third-generation radar; forward-looking infrared imagers; active radio frequency identification tags that can be queried at standoff ranges; and digital line-of-sight hazard markers.
- **Passive marking tools.** Passive tools include combat identification panels that provide a contrast against a vehicle hull, cloth thermal identification panels, infrared strobe lights, dismounted combat identification marking devices, highly reflective markers to identify battlefield hazards and noncombat sensitive sites; individual glow tape; and infrared helmet markers. The passive capabilities are enhanced by night vision equipment, long-range optics, close combat optics, vehicle fire control systems, and vehicle thermal viewers.
- **Training tools.** Virtual and live training tools include conduct-of-fire trainers, close combat tactical training systems, active targets, and vehicle recognition systems.

B-8. Technologies include, but are not limited to, the following:

- The Joint Combat Identification Marking System consists of combat identification panels, cloth thermal identification panels, infrared strobe lights, dismounted combat identification marking systems, individual glow tape, and infrared helmet markers.
- The U.S. military has many units equipped with differing combat identification capabilities. Although commanders know the capabilities within their command, the challenge is to integrate these capabilities across echelons to complement ROE.

AIR TO SURFACE

B-9. Air-to-surface combat identification begins after detecting an object and ends with exchanging information between the detectors and the shooter. Major tasks in air-to-surface combat identification include—

- Detecting objects in the AO.
- Locating object positions.

- Identifying the object as friendly, enemy, neutral, or unknown. If unknown, personnel continue identification procedures until determining object characteristics or they shift to another target if there is no immediate threat.
- Classifying information relevant to the targeted enemy. Personnel categorize the target in relation to the level of danger it represents. The proximity of friendly and neutral entities in relation to an identified target may impact the decision to engage due to second- or third-order effects, such as blast or rubble damage.
- Confirming the initial identification and classification of the target.
- Providing and verifying the information exchange to and from the shooter.

B-10. Achieving these tasks requires a weapons platform that can—
- Detect, locate, and identify the potential target before engaging it.
- Receive situational awareness on the target and the relevant target area, including friendly, enemy, and neutral entities.
- Communicate with a controller, such as an observer on the target or a C2 node. The controller quickly transmits relevant information in an easily understood format before target engagement.
- Engage the target.
- Assist with target assessment.

B-11. Air-to-surface attacks begin by a request from a ground or aerial observer. When an attack is initiated by a ground observer, friendly forces may be close to enemy targets, thus requiring clear target identification. Personnel mark friendly and enemy locations by multiple means when operating under dangerously close conditions. Aerial and ground combatants should agree that they understand the location of all relevant forces before engagement. (See figure B-2.) Some aircraft, such as the AC-130, can paint a target with infrared before engagement so that a ground observer can verify the target identification.

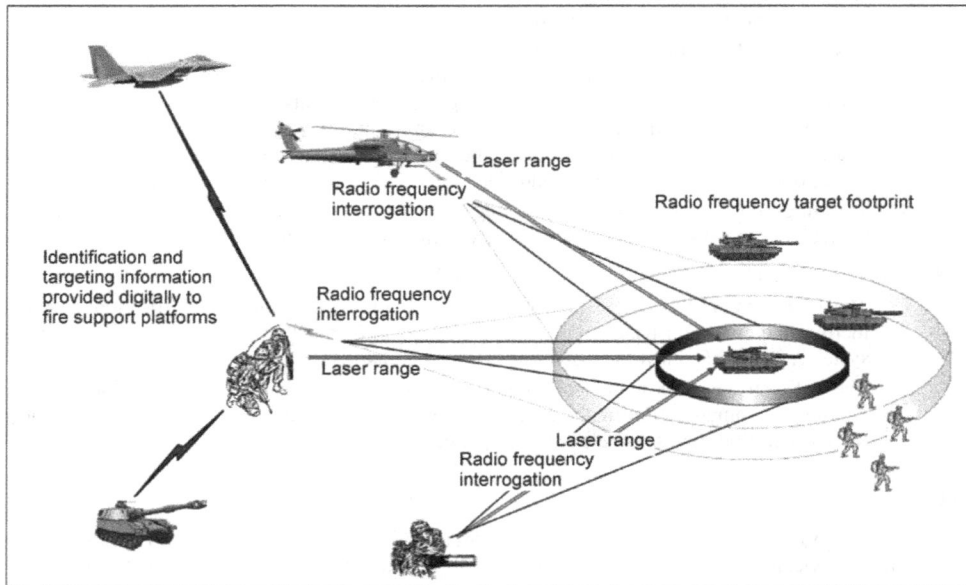

Figure B-2. Multiple target identification

B-12. Before initiation by an aerial platform, the pilot already has situational awareness and situational understanding of the target and surrounding target area. A pilot engages a target only after accessing all available knowledge providers and obtaining a positive visual confirmation.

B-13. Other air-to-surface considerations include the following:

- Combat identification features that ground forces can easily identify are not always as identifiable from an aviation platform.
- The Target Identification Panel System is a thermal, tape-marked cloth that mounts atop a vehicle. This surface-to-air identification device has limited surface-to-surface utility.
- Terminal attack controller training and equipment fully integrates with ground forces to ensure teamwork and understanding.
- Ground observers use a geographic designation system visible to aerial platforms.
- Communication links connect all aircraft and ground forces when maneuvering and fighting, including during darkness and limited visibility. Ground forces can "see" each other using Blue Force Tracker and are better able to avoid fratricide. All aircraft is not capable of interrogating a ground target as friendly before a lethal engagement occurs. One option is to pair the aircraft with a C2 aircraft that is equipped with Blue Force Tracker to quickly clear targets for engagement. If an aircraft lacks a combat identification system, leaders ensure that SOPs compel pilots to contact ground elements for aircraft clearance before engaging.

SURFACE TO AIR

B-14. Preventing enemy aerial attack is the responsibility of all joint force components. The correct identification of airspace users protects the force from enemy air attack and the erroneous engagement of friendly aircraft. *Identification, friend or foe* (IFF) is a device that emits a signal positively identifying it as friendly. (JP 1-02) (See FM 44-100 for more information.) It is the primary means of identifying friendly or unknown aerial platforms at an extended distance. Training must emphasize IFF procedures, manual identification procedures when IFF is not available, and the coordination requirements and procedures for engaging threats while protecting friendly aircraft. One technology used for IFF is the Mark XII (Mode 4), the current air-to-air and surface-to-air identification system that consists of a transponder on aircraft and an interrogator on air defense artillery sensors.

B-15. Army and other forces (joint, coalition, multinational) use airspace to conduct air operations, deliver fires, conduct air defense operations, and conduct intelligence operations. AC2 is the Army's operational approach to integrate airspace users and maximize the effectiveness of systems, while minimizing risks to friendly aircraft. By maintaining complete situational awareness of airspace users, AC2 enables early identification and coordinated air defense engagements of threat aircraft to prevent aerial attacks of friendly forces.

B-16. AC2 does not denote that any airspace contiguous to the AO or other geographical dimension of airspace is designated "Army" airspace. Neither does it imply command of any asset that is not assigned or under operational control to an Army commander. Under joint doctrine, airspace is not owned in the sense that assignment of an AO confers ownership of the ground. Airspace is used by multiple components and the joint force commander designates an airspace control authority (usually the joint force airspace control authority) to manage airspace.

B-17. AC2 personnel can effectively integrate Army, joint, and multinational airspace users operating within the ground commander's AO by maintaining complete situational awareness of the airspace, and maintaining communications with airspace users. As components of the Army Air Ground System, AC2 and AMD elements develop SOPs and annexes to facilitate AC2 and air defense operations that consistently follow joint procedures defined in JP 3-01, JP 3-30, JP 3-52, and the theater Airspace Control Plan:

- AMD and AC2 staff elements are organic to modular forces (brigade and higher).
- Multifunctional BCTs and support brigades (except sustainment) contain a version of an air defense airspace management (ADAM)/brigade aviation element (BAE) that is responsible for integrating brigade AC2, including AMD and aviation functions.

- Division and corps units contain an AC2 element in their main and tactical command posts.
- Numbered armies contain an AC2 element in their main and contingency command posts.
- The U.S. Army also has airspace managers as part of the battlefield coordination detachment, the combined arms liaison organization to the Air Operations Center.

Appendix C

Protection of Military Bases

Campaigning Armies have always required areas from which military operations and combat power can be supported, generated, and protected. These areas are generally known as FOBs, base camps, installations, or facilities. The static nature of these areas over time can lead to vulnerability of the force due to the inability to conduct offensive maneuver. Effective protection is generally achieved at these locations by developing protection strategies that utilize the forms and principles of protection and often benefit by collective security efforts with response forces.

PERMANENT BASES AND BASE CAMPS

C-1.   A *base* is a locality from which operations are projected or supported. (JP 1-02) Army bases overseas typically fall into two general categories: permanent bases (or installations) and base camps. A ***base camp*** **is an evolving military facility that supports the military operations of a deployed unit and provides the necessary support and services for sustained operations.** Base camps consist of intermediate staging bases and FOBs and support the tenants and equipment. While base camps are not permanent bases or installations, they develop many of the same functions and facilities the longer they exist. A base or base camp can contain one or more units from one or more Services. It has a defined perimeter and established access controls and takes advantage of natural and man-made features. Terrain around many permanent installations in CONUS, Korea, and Europe has changed since initial occupation; some installations lost initial terrain advantage due to urban growth and changes in the physical environment. This may present protection planning challenges in relation to standoff distances and traffic and access control.

C-2.   Generally, permanent bases are in host nations where the United States has a long-term lease agreement and a status-of-forces agreement. Intermediate staging bases are bases that are established near, but not in, the AO.

C-3.   A *FOB* is an area used to support tactical operations without establishing full support facilities. (FM 3-0). FOBs are located in friendly territory and are established to extend C2 or communications or to provide support for training and tactical operations. Commanders may establish a FOB for temporary or enduring operations. A FOB may include an airfield, unimproved airstrip, anchorage, or pier. FOBs range from small outposts to large, complex structures encompassing joint, interagency, and multinational forces. A large, intermediate staging base or FOB may require dedicated units, such as an MEB to serve as the base C2 headquarters and provide management for the protection warfighting function.

C-4.   Units often conduct operations from a FOB in a noncontiguous AO. These FOBs provide four key services: protection, critical infrastructure, C2, and sustainment. Whether establishing a FOB in Afghanistan, establishing an intermediate staging base in Iraq, or protecting an installation in Germany, leaders consider protection when planning mission accomplishment.

C-5.   Protecting bases and the units occupying the bases depends on units identifying and mitigating vulnerabilities based on the vulnerability assessment. Several levels of vulnerability assessments exist with varying degrees of scope and focus:

- **Higher headquarters assessment.** This is an overall assessment by a higher headquarters of how an organization is managing its AT program, including the management and compliance efforts by subordinate organizations. The higher headquarters assessment can include a joint staff-integrated vulnerability assessment.
- **Local assessment.** Local assessments are conducted by installation or unit AT officers, using key force protection working group members as the assessment team in a collaborative effort.

- **Specialized assessment.** Specialized assessments include assessments that are specifically aimed to test base defenses and assessments that are directed by commanders to assess specific threat capabilities.

C-6. Vulnerability assessments help base and unit commanders identify weaknesses, inefficiencies, and enhancements in security and protection programs. They need to be continuous and identify areas where protection efforts and resources should be focused.

C-7. Commanders are responsible for protecting military bases. They consider the twelve protection tasks and systems when developing military base protection plans.

AIR AND MISSILE DEFENSE CONSIDERATIONS

C-8. Air and missile attacks can pose significant threats to units in the AO. Bases in the AO often protect themselves from enemy air threats with passive air defense measures. Base commanders are responsible for base defense. Most bases lack support from short-range air defense systems. Instead, they receive protection from high-to-medium altitude missile air defense systems. Base commanders do not normally control positioning of these systems since they are a theater level asset. However, base and unit commanders ensure that they have adequate air defense procedures in place to defend their units and bases.

C-9. Air defense commanders have the authority to establish local ADWs that are higher but not lower than the ADW established by the area air defense commander. An early warning alerts units and bases to a possible air attack before it occurs. Commanders identify threat aircraft early enough to sound the local warning system. Base commanders ensure that the base defense operations center receives information and warnings from the air battle management operations center. Base commanders prepare units to face an air threat with no supporting air defense artillery.

C-10. During an air threat, bases and units comply with passive air defense measures. Base and unit commanders address passive air defense measures in SOPs at all levels and develop a routine to implement these measures. Hazard assessment includes analyzing enemy air activity. This analysis drives the implementation of select measures. For example, if enemy air activity is likely to occur during the day only, most movement should occur during hours of limited visibility. Passive air defense measures become more significant when changes in ADWs exist. Units follow specific passive air defense measures if defense systems issue a notification of imminent enemy air attack.

C-11. Some bases may have a dedicated, indirect-fire protection capability, including a base targeting surveillance system. The base defense operations center often controls this asset. Indirect-fire protection intercept systems, like all air defense artillery systems, cannot protect all base assets and personnel with 100 percent surety. Therefore, commanders prioritize which assets receive dedicated, indirect-fire protection.

FRATRICIDE AVOIDANCE CONSIDERATIONS

C-12. Fratricide can occur anywhere on the battlefield, including bases. Unit commanders must have a plan to reduce the risk of friendly fire that results in fratricide. Key fratricide avoidance principles include—

- **Control measures.** Commanders distribute adequate control measures to the lowest level.
- **Operation concept.** Commanders ensure that all Soldiers understand the commander's concept of operation and that of adjacent units. When operating from FOBs in large urban environments, units remain aware of operational friendly forces and NGOs in the AO.
- **Rehearsal.** Commanders ensure that Soldiers understand the operation and rehearse the plan to become familiar with the unit orientation during the mission.
- **Navigation devices.** Soldiers need to become familiar with and use available navigation devices to avoid becoming lost or disoriented. SOPs ensure that lost or disoriented units know how to immediately contact higher headquarters for instructions and assistance.
- **Common operational picture updates.** Units and Soldiers constantly update their operational picture to keep up with changes to enemy and friendly situations.

- **Positive identification.** Leaders ensure that Soldiers make positive identification before engaging targets.
- **Visual identification panels.** Units mark vehicles so that other friendly units operating in the area can identify them.
- **ROE.** Commanders ensure that Soldiers clearly understand the ROE.

OPERATIONAL AREA SECURITY CONSIDERATIONS

C-13. Commanders establish bases for a defined mission or purpose, and the base location should support that mission or purpose. When considering a base location, commanders select a site that they can defend, not one that is convenient. Units often operate without a well-defined support area. In some cases, support units are not colocated with combat units. This means that support units are centrally located in the AO and have to provide their own security. (See FMI 2-01.301 for more information.) Base locations also benefit from established lines of communications that are sustainable and defensible. To maximize protection, commanders select base locations based on OAKOC.

C-14. All bases are designed and manned to defeat Level I and Level II threats. Three levels of threat categories exist:

- **Level I**—a small enemy force that can be defeated by a unit's organic resources.
- **Level II**—an enemy activity that requires the commitment of a reaction force to defeat it.
- **Level III**—a threat that requires the commitment of a TCF to defeat it.

C-15. In some operations and areas, a conventional force, Level III threat (insurgents that have consolidated to form a Level III threat) may exist. In these situations, the base response force or mobile security force engages the Level III threat until another response force or TCF arrives to help defeat the enemy. (See JP 3-10 for more information.)

BASE COMMANDER

C-16. A base commander—

- Integrates the protection warfighting elements to protect and secure personnel, physical assets, and information.
- May appoint a base defense force commander to help execute base defense functions. (The base defense force commander tasks units to provide Soldiers and materiel needed to form a base defense force.)
- Organizes the base defense force as required by the threat assessment and the types of units located on or near the base.
- Requests support from specialized forces (EOD, CBRN reconnaissance) if required.

BASE DEFENSE OPERATIONS CENTER

C-17. The base defense operations center is a C2 facility. The base commander establishes the center to serve as the focal point for base security and defense. It plans, directs, integrates, coordinates, and controls all base defense efforts. If the base commander is a battalion commander, the base defense operations center forms on the nucleus provided by the battalion staff. On large bases with multiple units conducting varied missions, the base defense operations center consists of units tasked with base defense responsibilities.

C-18. A *base cluster* in base defense operations is a collection of bases, geographically grouped for mutual protection and ease of C2. (JP 3-10) A base cluster normally lacks a defined perimeter or established access points. The base cluster commander and base cluster operations center provide C2 to multiple bases and integrate protection efforts and defense plans.

BASE DEFENSE FORCE

C-19. *Base defense forces* are troops assigned or attached to a base for the primary purpose of base defense and security as well as augmentees and selectively armed personnel available to the base commander for base defense from units performing primary missions other than base defense. (JP 3-10) This security element provides local perimeter security and base defense. It may consist of one unit or a combination of units assigned to the base. It consists of the guard force, which may include static or roving elements comprised of joint, multinational, host nation, contracted security, or quick-reaction forces based on the mission variables. The quick-reaction force often has a squad- to platoon-size element located on the base. It reinforces the guard force in the event of a Level I or Level II attack.

MOBILE SECURITY FORCE

C-20. The *mobile security force* is a dedicated security force designed to defeat Level I and Level II threats on a base and/or base cluster. (JP 3-10) A platoon- or company-size mobile security force may be assigned to one base, but may support multiple bases. Regardless, planners incorporate the mobile security force into the base defense plan. These units reinforce threatened areas, block enemy penetrations of primary security positions, and counterattack. They often arrive as mechanized or motorized elements with armor protection. The mobile security force "shapes" a Level III threat until a TCF arrives that is capable of destroying armor-protected vehicles and dismounted infantry.

PROTECTION CONSIDERATIONS

C-21. Base AT protection requires the close cooperation and integration of activities, units, and planning. Most failures to protect bases from terrorist attacks can be attributed to the failure of various organizations to coordinate activities, share responsibilities, and disseminate intelligence information.

C-22. The same principles of defense apply to base AT protection. Considerations for access to the base perimeter and various clusters, effective communications, control measures, and integrated barrier systems play an important role in building necessary protection against prospective terrorist attacks.

C-23. Contracting is often part of base defense. Base defense responsibilities should include necessary checks on contracts. Whether the contract involves products (food, water, construction) or personnel (contracted guards, workers) it should be vetted through a system which ensures that AT considerations are taken into account.

ACCESS CONTROL

C-24. Thorough base protection includes identification checks of all personnel entering bases in high-threat areas. The proper vetting of host nation support and contract personnel enhances security. Incorporating random AT measures into the access control plan varies the level of detail required for access. This keeps the guard force alert and keeps the enemy off balance. Additional identification measures (biometrics, metal detectors, X-ray devices) are critical to effective access control.

PERIMETER DEFENSE

C-25. An effective and alert base defense force best deters Level I and Level II threats. Adequate standoff distances from buildings and other structures outside the perimeter greatly enhance perimeter defense. An accurate threat assessment, combined with defense in depth, helps determine the standoff distance required. The staff EOD or engineer can help determine the appropriate standoff distances to protect against blasts from IEDs. Random patrols inside and outside the perimeter (as part of the base random AT measures and direct-fire positions on key access points and critical locations) also enhance security. In addition, some strategies randomly use countersurveillance teams to defeat enemy surveillance.

PROTECTION AND DEFENSE IN DEPTH

C-26. Protection and defense in depth include available friendly forces and physical barriers. Both should be deployed in depth, in a concentric fashion, to allow maximum protection. The base defense force deploys physical barriers in depth beginning with the perimeter fence line. It also clears fields of fire and uses barriers and other entry control measures to control pedestrian and vehicle egress from and ingress to the base. The base defense force uses barriers to protect critical assets and infrastructures inside the base.

AIR BASE APPROACH AND DEPARTURE CORRIDOR SECURITY

C-27. Aircraft are especially vulnerable when operating in the "low and slow" takeoff and landing flight regimes. Airbase approach and departure corridor security operations protect aircraft from shoulder-launched, surface-to-air threats when they take off and land at airbases. Base commanders of any Service who command installations with active airfields identify considerations for planning and securing air operations that are subject to threat systems. This includes approach and departure corridors used by the aircraft. (See JP 3-10 for more information.)

CONTROL MEASURES

C-28. Control measures in base defense operations resemble those used in other defense operations. The area commander establishes base boundaries in coordination with the base or base cluster commander. Area, base, and base cluster commanders coordinate base boundaries and establish phase lines, contact points, objectives, and checkpoints that are necessary to control base clusters. The base boundary is not necessarily the base perimeter. Rather, it is established on the mission variables, specifically balancing the need of the base defense forces to control key terrain with their ability to accomplish the mission. The base boundary may or may not be contiguous to other base AOs. Commanders may further subdivide the unit's assigned area into subordinate AOs, bases, and base clusters and assign maneuver forces to assembly areas and battle positions. They establish fire support coordination measures to permit or restrict fires in and around the base. (See FM 3-09.32 for more information.) No-fire areas may be required to protect civilians; prevent the disruption of sustaining operations; or protect combat outposts, observation posts, and patrols from friendly fire. Commanders coordinate all established control graphics with host nation organizations to minimize interference, misunderstandings, and collateral damage. The base defense force commander (in coordination with the base commander) designates the base perimeter, target reference points, and sectors of fire to organizations located at the base.

PHYSICAL SECURITY, BARRIER, AND SURVIVABILITY PLAN

C-29. Commanders use obstacles to provide Soldiers, equipment, facilities, and supplies with a level of survivability in the event of an attack or attempted attack. Obstacles can be categorized as tactical or protective:

- **Tactical.** Tactical obstacles directly attack the enemy's ability to move, mass, and reinforce.
- **Protective.** Protective obstacles provide close-in protection for the friendly force and are categorized as hasty or deliberate. They range from tetrahedrons and concrete barriers to networked munitions.

C-30. Physical barriers provide a protection capability and are available in many forms; some are inexpensive and flexible (such as tetrahedrons), and others are resource-intensive and inflexible (such as walls). Networked munitions replace conventional mines and provide a rapidly emplaced intrusion detection and denial system for base and perimeter security. These munitions are remotely controlled from a central station and provide scalable, lethal and nonlethal effects. The base survivability plan includes other measures of hardening and the construction of supporting structures, such as entry control points and guard towers.

EARLY WARNING SYSTEM

C-31. All bases should have an electronic and audio early warning system that personnel on the base can understand. For an effective defense, bases rehearse immediate battle drills to protect Soldiers and units.

SURVIVABILITY AND BARRIER CONSIDERATIONS

C-32. The development of a base and the ability to defend it relies on the innovation, adaptability, and use of engineer assets. Local contractors often make up for shortages in organic equipment and personnel. Commercial engineer equipment can often provide the greatest versatility throughout base development and maintenance.

C-33. Commanders construct protective shelters and defensive positions to protect Soldiers from direct and indirect fire and explosives. They might modify existing structures to meet survivability needs. Units construct structurally sound fighting positions under the supporting engineer's supervision. The supporting engineer determines the required construction materials and whether the positions meet safety considerations.

C-34. Reduced vulnerability to explosives occurs if units establish adequate perimeters and move critical areas as far from the perimeter as practical. Standoff distances and window protection reduce blast effects. The supporting engineers can determine adequate standoff distances based on the threat.

C-35. All barrier plans include measures to block high-speed avenues of approach to the entrance and high-risk targets.

> *Note.* See United Facilities Criteria (UFC) 4-010-01, UFC 4-010-02, UFC 4-022-01, FM 5-103, and GTA 90-01-010, *Joint Contingency Operations Base Force Protection Handbook* for more information.

FORCE HEALTH PROTECTION CONSIDERATIONS

C-36. Base commanders are responsible for protecting the health of their Soldiers. One of the most important FHP considerations is ensuring the quality of base food and water supplies. Base commanders develop procedures to protect these supplies from environmental threats and intentional tampering. Otherwise, personnel may risk exposure to harmful levels of contaminants, such as physical hazards, TIM, radiation, or biological agents. Harmful levels of contaminants can be high-level or low-level exposures:

- **High-level exposure.** High-level exposure results in immediate health effects.
- **Low-level exposure.** Low-level exposure results in delayed, long-term effects.

C-37. Base and unit commanders use the Army's CRM process to evaluate risks posed by hazards. Through the protection cell, a commander can implement a specific team that looks at food and water security. A multidisciplinary approach systematically reviews and assesses food systems. This team consists of—

- Protection officer.
- Preventive medicine officer.
- Veterinary corps officer.
- Unit food advisor.
- Provost marshal representative.
- Military intelligence representative.

C-38. The exact process for the base and unit food and water security program varies. The program depends on information such as base or unit type, location, and size; distribution chain; and personnel involved. The protection working group considers the unique conditions of each food system when developing a program. The group evaluates food supply and distribution systems for current safety and security operations. After developing initial procedures, the protection working group completes periodic reviews to validate vulnerabilities and verifies and updates the program assumptions, guidelines, and restrictions.

CHEMICAL, BIOLOGICAL, RADIOLOGICAL, AND NUCLEAR CONSIDERATIONS

C-39. Base commanders coordinate CBRN defense of their base and of bases designated in their AO. The base commander and the protection staff identify the CBRN threat and notify units and at-risk civilians of the threat. They recommend appropriate training and early warning measures based on the threat, assess readiness and vulnerabilities, and identify CBRN defense requirements. Defensive planning should account for likely transient units that may only occupy the base for a short term. (See FM 3-11.34 for more information.)

C-40. Base commanders ensure that CBRN defense planning integrates closely with AMD planning. They consider that threat missile delivery systems range from mortars to surface-to-surface missiles. (See the following vignette.)

CBRN Defense

On 27 March 2003, an Iraqi surface-to-surface missile was launched against coalition forces at Camp Doha, Kuwait. PATRIOT missile batteries successfully intercepted the inbound missile 7 kilometers east of Camp Doha, headquarters of the Combined Forces Land Component Command, which controlled ground forces involved in Operation Iraqi Freedom.

About 90 minutes later, an unknown biological agent triggered several aerosol sensors within the Mishref District of Kuwait City. The sensors were the first line of defense and could detect biological agents with particles of a certain size. The Czech contingent of the task force deployed a biological sampling team. The team determined the agents to be Escherichia coli (E. coli) bacteria, which the team believed to be the result of high winds blowing the bacteria from an unregulated dump near Kuwait City. Since the alarms were sounded on the basis of a missile attack, Kuwaiti officials issued a warning to residents in Mishref to stay in their homes or to don protective masks. Once the Czech analysts gave the all clear, Kuwaitis went about their business.

SAFETY CONSIDERATIONS

C-41. The proper storage of arms and ammunition critically affects mission accomplishment and the safety of deployed Soldiers. Even in high-threat areas, where renewed combat operations can happen, base protection requires properly stored arms and ammunition.

C-42. A significant loss of combat power resulted from the Camp Doha explosion shown in the following vignette. This incident nearly destroyed an entire squadron and sharply reduced the regiment's overall combat power. Logisticians estimated total losses at more $40 million.

Improper Storage of Arms and Ammunition **Causes Damage and Destruction**
In June 1991, four months after Operation Desert Storm ended, the 11th Armored Cavalry Regiment (ACR) deployed from Germany to occupy Camp Doha, Kuwait, and serve as a deterrent and rapid response force. By July 1991, the 11th ACR was the only U.S. ground combat unit remaining in the Gulf Theater. Due to the threat of renewed hostilities, the 11th ACR kept its combat vehicles "combat loaded" with ammunition while in garrison. The regiment stored an equal amount of ammunition in military vans (containers) located in the north compound motor pool complex near the combat vehicle parking ramps.
On the morning of 11 July 1991, the 11th ACR deployed two of its three combat formations to the field, leaving behind a single squadron to serve as a guard force. The squadron was parked in Camp Doha's north compound. This fenced-off area contained several motor pool pads, some administrative buildings, a wash rack, and living quarters for about 250 British soldiers.
At approximately 1020 hours, a defective heater in an M992 ammunition carrier caught on fire. The carrier was loaded with 155-millimeter artillery shells. Troops unsuccessfully tried to extinguish the fire before being ordered to evacuate the north compound. This evacuation was still underway when the burning M992 exploded at 1100 hours, scattering artillery submunitions over nearby, combat-loaded vehicles and ammunition stocks.
This set off an hours-long series of explosions and fires that devastated vehicles and equipment in the north compound and scattered UXO and debris over much of the camp. The fires produced billowing clouds of smoke that rose hundreds of feet into the air and drifted across portions of the north and south compounds, in the direction of Kuwait City.
By midafternoon, the fires had died down enough to allow a preliminary damage assessment. There were no fatalities; however, 49 Soldiers were injured, 2 seriously. Most injuries were fractures, sprains, contusions, or lacerations suffered when Soldiers scrambled over the 15-foot-high perimeter wall. The destruction was overwhelming. The fire and explosions damaged or destroyed 102 vehicles, including 4 M1A1 tanks and other combat vehicles, and more than 2 dozen buildings sustained damage. The fires destroyed about $15 million worth of ammunition and highlighted the importance of having ammunition supply point accident cleanup procedures in place

OPERATIONS SECURITY CONSIDERATIONS

C-43. OPSEC is vital to protecting information. In addition to protecting classified information, a good OPSEC program denies the enemy access to unclassified, critical information about friendly forces. This critical information could allow an enemy to delay or disrupt friendly plans, operations, or missions; determine the base commander's next move; or assess base vulnerabilities, weaknesses, and strengths. Examples of a weakness or vulnerability include—

- Perimeter surveillance cameras not working properly.
- Perimeter gates malfunctioning.
- Guard force reductions.
- Communications vulnerabilities.
- Access control vulnerabilities.

C-44. The base or unit OPSEC officer works with the AT officer to create a CAL. The CAL changes according to the threat environment, and commanders adjust it periodically. They brief it only to appropriate personnel in a need-to-know status.

CONTRACTOR PERSONNEL CONSIDERATIONS

C-45. Commanders consider protection as it pertains to contractor personnel. Commanders decide whether to use contractors and then determine whether to use U.S. contractors. The type of contractor employed affects protection considerations. (See the following vignette.)

Coordinating Non-DOD Contractor Support

In many contingencies, Army commanders coordinate with the DOS or other government agencies to integrate non-DOD contractor support into the overall joint security plan. For example, during Operation Iraqi Freedom, DOS coordinated directly with Multinational Force–Iraq. This coordination properly integrated major DOS-sponsored reconstruction efforts into the military security plan. Such efforts included DOS-funded, contracted security forces. Protection requirements became so challenging that commanders created a combined DOS-DOD contracting coordination center. This center provided the necessary planning capabilities, information sharing, and coordination measures. It directly linked regional reconstruction coordination centers into area commander operations centers. These regional coordination centers provided area commanders with key information on DOS missions being conducted in their AOs. This critical information assisted area commanders when they provided backup security support to DOS missions, facilities, and personnel.

C-46. From the base security perspective, commanders carefully consider using local or third-country national employees. In some operational situations, using such personnel creates significant risks. The theater subordinate Army force planners and their contract oversight organizations assess the security risk of using local or third-country national personnel instead of U.S. contractors and military support capabilities. This assessment includes an analysis of security risks versus the negative strategic impact of not employing these personnel. Based on joint force and component commander decisions, base commanders conduct a local vulnerability assessment as it relates to using local or third-country national personnel. Answer the following questions when considering the use of local or third-country national employees to support base operations:

- Will contractor personnel reside on or off base? If they live off base, what base access control measures are required?
- How will access be controlled to specific areas within the base?
- Is there a vetting and badging process in place? If so, who will enforce it and how will it be enforced?
- Will contractor personnel be physically screened or searched in order to enter the base?
- Will armed escorts be required? If so, who will do this and how will it be resourced?
- Are special technologies (metal detectors, X-ray machines) needed and available?

C-47. Area, base, and supported unit commanders provide individual protection support. Sometimes, they provide security to contractors as determined by the Army force commander. To perform such tasks properly, area and base commanders maintain requisite visibility over supporting contingency contractors in their AOs.

Note. See FM 3-100.21 for more information.

This page intentionally left blank.

Appendix D

Operations Security

Leaders and Soldiers implement OPSEC as part of protection. OPSEC is not a collection of specific measures to apply to every operation; it is the part of the CRM process that protects information. OPSEC applies to all operations and activities at all levels of command.

OPERATIONS SECURITY APPLICATION

Note. See chapter 2 for a definition of OPSEC.

D-1.   OPSEC is how commanders manage risks to information. All units conduct (plan, prepare, execute, and continually assess) OPSEC to preserve essential secrecy. OPSEC is vital to the success of operations. Information that friendly forces take for granted is often what adversaries need to obtain defeat. Practicing effective OPSEC, however routine, denies adversaries information and protects friendly forces.

D-2.   Everyone must practice OPSEC and understand the cost of OPSEC compromises. It covers a range of activities, from avoiding predictable patterns of behavior to camouflaging equipment. Good OPSEC involves communicating why OPSEC is important and what Soldiers are supposed to accomplish. Understanding why they do something and what their actions are supposed to accomplish allows Soldiers to perform tasks more effectively. Successful OPSEC requires Soldiers to take deliberate and knowledgeable actions. (See AR 530-1 for more information.)

OPERATIONS SECURITY AS PART OF THE COMPOSITE RISK MANAGEMENT PROCESS

D-3.   The OPSEC officer helps the G-3 integrate OPSEC into the operations process. Risk management is an integral part of protection and the MDMP.

Note. See FM 5-19 for more information.

D-4.   Commanders practice OPSEC to protect information. OPSEC planning produces a set of coordinated OPSEC measures and tasks that Soldiers and units perform to protect the force. *OPSEC measures* **are methods and means to gain and maintain essential secrecy about EEFI.** Throughout the MDMP, the protection cell treats OPSEC measures as protection tasks. During orders production, planners incorporate OPSEC measures as protection tasks and tasks to subordinate units.

STEP 1. IDENTIFY HAZARDS

D-5.   The first step of OPSEC is to identify hazards. Hazards within the context of OPSEC are identified by analyzing the EFFI, the capability and intent of adversaries to collect EEFI, and friendly vulnerabilities that may aid enemy collection. Figure D-1, page D-2, shows how OPSEC integrates with the operations process and CRM.

	Operations Process Activity	Operations Security Action	Risk Management Step
ASSESSMENT	PLANNING	• Identify EEFI. • Analyze adversaries. • Analyze vulnerabilities. • Assess risk.	• Identify hazards. • Assess hazards. • Develop controls and make risk decisions.
	PREPARATION/ EXECUTION	• Apply appropriate OPSEC measures.	• Implement controls.
	ASSESSMENT		• Supervise and evaluate.

Figure D-1. Integration of OPSEC

Essential Elements of Friendly Information

D-6. The first element of hazard identification is to identify the EEFI. *EEFI* is the critical aspect of a friendly operation that, if known by the enemy, would subsequently compromise, lead to failure, or limit success of the operation, and, therefore, must be protected from enemy detection. (FM 3-0)

D-7. Identifying EEFI begins with the commander's initial guidance during mission receipt. The OPSEC officer recommends initial EEFI if the commander does not name any in the initial guidance. Several sources can help determine information to recommend as EEFI, such as—

- Commander's guidance.
- Intelligence estimate (information about the enemy and enemy intelligence intentions and capabilities).
- Counterintelligence estimate produced by the G-2 analysis and control element (normally an appendix to annex B of the OPORD or OPLAN or a tab to the intelligence estimate).
- Higher headquarters security classification guide for the operation. The security classification guide identifies classified information and EEFI related to the operation. It consists of sensitive information since it names (by classification level) the operation's most sensitive areas.
- Laws and executive orders that require protection of unclassified controlled information.

D-8. The staff identifies possible EEFI and submits them for command approval. Once approved, the staff develops OPSEC measures to shield EEFI from enemy collection systems. The EEFI differ from the CCIR; however, they are on the same level as CCIR since they are approved by the commander and covered in the base OPORD.

D-9. Facts, assumptions, and essential tasks may reveal EEFI that apply to the operation. In addition, each COA may have EEFI that apply only to it. As the staff war-games a COA, the G-2 identifies friendly information that, if known to adversaries, would allow them to counter the COA. The OPSEC officer adds these elements of information to the EEFI for that COA and records them in the running estimate. Upon COA approval, the EEFI for the approved COA become part of the EEFI for the operation.

D-10. When identifying EEFI, the OPSEC officer determines how long each element needs protection. Not all elements of information need protection for the duration of an operation. Some elements need protection only during specific events; others may not need protection until a branch or sequel is executed. Additional EEFI may be added during the execution of a COA because of circumstances that were unknown when the original EEFI were developed.

D-11. After identifying the EEFI, the OPSEC officer analyzes the enemy's capability and intent to collect friendly EEFI. The OPSEC officer also determines the enemy's potential to determine friendly vulnerabilities.

Enemy Capability and Intent

D-12. The second element of hazard identification is an analysis of the threat, summarized as most dangerous and most likely. The most dangerous situation occurs when an enemy has the capability (intelligence, surveillance, and reconnaissance assets) and intent to collect data from friendly vulnerabilities and is able to determine EEFI. The most likely situation stems from how the enemy used its assets during past operations. The G-2, G-3, and OPSEC officer analyze threat characteristics as part of IPB. Enemy intentions and collection capabilities are identified by asking the following questions:

- Who are the adversaries?
- Who has the intent and capabilities to act against the planned operation?
- What are probable enemy objectives?
- What are likely enemy actions against friendly operations?
- What information do adversaries already know?
- What collection capabilities do adversaries possess or have access to by financial arrangement, shared ideologies, or coordinated coalitions or alliances?
- Which OPSEC indicators can be faked to deceive adversaries?

Friendly Vulnerabilities

D-13. The final element of hazard identification is to determine OPSEC vulnerabilities of an operation or activity. It has two parts—identify OPSEC indicators and identify OPSEC vulnerabilities.

- **OPSEC indicator.** An OPSEC indicator is a friendly detectable action or open-source information that an enemy can interpret or piece together to derive EEFI. The G-2, G-3, and OPSEC officer examine all aspects and phases of the operation to find OPSEC indicators. Then, they compare them with the enemy targeting cycle and collection capabilities, considering these questions:
  - What OPSEC indicators will friendly forces create during the operation?
  - What OPSEC indicators can the enemy actually collect?
  - What OPSEC indicators will the enemy be able to use to the disadvantage of friendly forces?

Note. The answers to these questions identify OPSEC vulnerabilities.

- **OPSEC vulnerability.** An OPSEC vulnerability is a condition in which friendly actions provide OPSEC indicators that may be obtained and accurately evaluated by an enemy in time to provide a basis for effective enemy decisionmaking. An OPSEC vulnerability exists when a threat can collect information from an OPSEC indicator, correctly analyze the information, make a decision, and take timely action to degrade friendly operations or place itself in an advantage over friendly forces. Analyzing OPSEC vulnerabilities continues through all phases of the operations process.

D-14. An OPSEC officer abides by the following methodology:

- Examine each part of the operation, in coordination with the intelligence staff and other staff elements, to find actions or information that will provide indicators in each area (human resources, logistics, communications, movement activities, aviation).
- Compare the identified indicators with threat intelligence collection capabilities. One method is to develop a mission timeline and identify anything along the timeline that the commander wants protected.
- Ensure that participants identify actions along the timeline that must be accomplished for the mission to be accomplished.
- Identify which must-be-accomplished actions can be indicators that a threat could use. Compare each indicator with each threat collection capability. Where there is a match, there is vulnerability.

D-15. An OPSEC vulnerability is a type of hazard related to EEFI. Unprotected OPSEC vulnerabilities entail risk. CRM allows the OPSEC officer to integrate risk assessments from OPSEC vulnerabilities with assessments of other risks. The OPSEC officer records OPSEC vulnerabilities and further analyzes them during the next step.

STEP 2. ASSESS HAZARDS

D-16. The OPSEC officer begins hazard assessment by analyzing the OPSEC vulnerabilities identified during mission analysis and COA development and then identifies possible OPSEC measures for each one. The OPSEC officer concurrently assesses the risks posed by existing threats and OPSEC vulnerabilities. This assessment has four parts:

- Complete a hazard assessment for each OPSEC vulnerability.
- Select one or more OPSEC measures to counter the OPSEC vulnerability.
- Determine residual risk for each OPSEC vulnerability.
- Decide which OPSEC measures to implement.

D-17. Some OPSEC measures may protect more than one OPSEC vulnerability. During assessment, the OPSEC officer evaluates the sufficiency of standard security measures. This evaluation covers such areas as personnel, physical, cryptographic, document, special access, and automated information systems security and may include an OPSEC review. Continuing OPSEC measures in these areas may protect some OPSEC vulnerabilities.

D-18. The OPSEC officer determines the residual risk for each OPSEC vulnerability after applying the appropriate OPSEC measures. Residual risk is the level of risk remaining after controls have been identified and selected for hazards. In this context, OPSEC measures are controls.

Note. See FM 5-19 for more information.

STEP 3. DEVELOP CONTROLS AND MAKE RISK DECISIONS

D-19. Risk assessment drives the development of appropriate controls to mitigate the risk. Planners strive to develop OPSEC measures that shield OPSEC vulnerabilities and require the fewest resources. The most desirable OPSEC measures provide the needed protection at the least cost to operational effectiveness.

D-20. OPSEC measures come in three forms:

- **Action control.** Action control eliminates indicators or the vulnerability of actions to exploitation by threat intelligence systems. OPSEC officers select the actions to undertake; decide whether to execute actions (Weblog restrictions, trash control, mandatory use of secure communications, OPSEC reviews); and determine the "who," "when," "where," and "how" that are necessary to accomplish the actions.
- **Countermeasures.** Countermeasures disrupt effective threat information gathering or prevent their recognition of indicators when processing collected materials. OPSEC officers use diversions, camouflage, concealment, jamming, threats, police powers, and force against threat information gathering and processing capabilities as countermeasures.
- **Counteranalysis.** Counteranalysis is accomplished by using deception techniques, and it prevents accurate interpretations of indicators during threat analysis of collected materials.

D-21. The OPSEC officer develops proposed OPSEC measures based on the hazard assessment. The cell compares the residual risk with the risk posed by the OPSEC vulnerability if the OPSEC measure is not executed. The difference forms an estimate of the benefit gained from the OPSEC measure. In deciding which OPSEC measures to recommend, staffs consider questions such as—

- What is the cost in terms of combat power if an OPSEC measure is employed?
- Does the cost jeopardize mission success? The OPSEC officer may recommend a no-measures alternative if cost outweighs the risk.
- What is the risk to mission success if an OPSEC measure is not executed?
- What is the risk to mission success if an OPSEC measure fails?

D-22. The OPSEC officer coordinates OPSEC measures as they are developed to minimize redundancy and ensure that they do not create new OPSEC indicators. The OPSEC officer double-checks these factors during the COA analysis. Coordination requirements may include—

- Determining the effects of some OPSEC measures on public affairs operations.
- Obtaining guidance on the termination of OPSEC measures.

- Obtaining guidance on the declassification and public release of OPSEC-related activities.
- Obtaining administrative and logistics support for OPSEC tasks.
- Establishing OPSEC coordination and C2 measures.
- Establishing assessment (monitoring and evaluation) mechanisms.
- Submitting requests for information to support the assessment of protection tasks and systems.
- Conducting OPSEC checks.
- Arranging input for after-action reviews.
- Arranging support of OPSEC-related communications requirements.

STEP 4. IMPLEMENT CONTROLS

D-23. The OPSEC officer submits appropriate OPSEC measures for command approval. These measures may entail significant expenditures of time, resources, or personnel. Commanders normally approve OPSEC measures during the COA approval. Approved OPSEC measures become OPSEC tasks. The OPSEC officer determines the MOEs and MOPs for the OPSEC tasks, ensures that the OPLAN or OPORD includes them, and arranges to assess them throughout preparation and execution. The G-3 directs the execution of OPSEC measures through warning orders, OPORDs, or fragmentary orders.

D-24. After the commander approves OPSEC measures, the OPSEC officer monitors their implementation and evaluates their MOP and MOE. The OPSEC officer adjusts measures, if necessary, based on this assessment. The OPSEC officer coordinates the monitoring of OPSEC measures with the G-2 and counterintelligence staffs so that the measures receive appropriate priority. Monitoring may generate information requests, and the OPSEC officer passes these requests to the G-2 for inclusion in the collection plan. Some requests may become priority information requirements.

D-25. Commanders continuously maintain OPSEC. Assessing OPSEC measures includes collecting lessons learned. Most lessons arise while monitoring the execution of OPSEC measures, but others arise from an evaluation of a completed operation or program.

STEP 5. SUPERVISE AND EVALUATE

D-26. OPSEC measures are supervised and evaluated continuously throughout the operations process. Protection cell members stay alert for OPSEC indicators in their functional areas that may result in OPSEC vulnerabilities. Continuous assessment contributes to refining OPSEC products.

Operations Security Review

D-27. The OPSEC review evaluates information or visual products to protect EEFI. A reviewed product may be, but is not limited to, memorandums, e-mails, articles, academic papers, videos, briefings, contracts, news releases, technical documents, plans, orders, responses to the Freedom of Information Act, Privacy Act requests, Web pages, weblogs, or other visual or electronic media. ARs require the OPSEC officer to review products related to U.S. government or military operations and other supporting programs before release in the public domain. An OPSEC review is normally conducted with a public affairs review for the release of official information to the public.

D-28. All staff sections review documents and automated information system logs to protect sensitive information. SOPs should state which documents (news releases, Web pages, responses to Freedom of Information Act and Privacy Act requests) automatically go to the OPSEC officer for review. They should also provide standards for protecting, storing, and handling sensitive information and information systems. When corrective action is necessary, such as an OPSEC assessment or review, the OPSEC officer provides recommendations to the appropriate staff officer.

Operations Security Assessment

D-29. OPSEC assessments monitor an operation to determine the unit's overall OPSEC posture. They evaluate compliance of subordinate organizations with the OPSEC program, plan, or guidance. OPSEC officers conduct OPSEC assessments and submit results and recommendations to the commander. They normally assess the—

- Identification of EEFI.
- Unit personnel knowledge of EEFI.
- Unit personnel knowledge of the collection threat.
- OPSEC measures in place to protect identified critical information.

D-30. The following are some questions that OPSEC officers should ask to determine the status of OPSEC in the command:

- How often did subordinate commanders change daily movement plans?
- How many times did commanders conduct similar attack patterns consecutively?
- How many elements of EEFI were covered by two or more OPSEC measures?
- How many collection efforts were targeted against EEFI?
- How vulnerable was the friendly plan?
- How many friendly OPSEC vulnerabilities were exploited by threat action?
- How many times did threat detection disrupt friendly operations?
- How many support facilities were protected from threat observation?
- How many friendly operational movements were observed by threat overhead surveillance?
- How often did OPSEC and deception planners coordinate actions?
- How many OPSEC measures were selected based on the vulnerability analysis?
- How many times did OPSEC planners have access to compartmented planning efforts?
- How many times was OPSEC guidance received from higher headquarters?
- Was the timing or location of routine actions changed at least weekly?
- How many units were equipped with antisurveillance sensor and sensor jamming devices?

Operations Security Survey

D-31. The OPSEC officer completes the OPSEC survey in coordination with other staff members. This survey determines if the command adequately protects EEFI. It analyzes the conduct of the operation to identify sources of information, what the command discloses, and what can be derived from the information. It aims to identify unprotected OPSEC vulnerabilities and helps the commander assess OPSEC measures and adjust them if necessary.

D-32. Effective OPSEC surveys are resource-intensive and require careful planning, thorough data collection, and thoughtful analysis. The OPSEC officer conducts surveys only when deemed necessary by the commander and may execute an informal assessment to determine if a complete OPSEC survey is needed.

Note. See AR 530-1 for more information.

Operations Security Estimate

D-33. The OPSEC officer maintains a running estimate to help supervise and evaluate OPSEC. A *running estimate* is a staff section's continuous assessment of current and future operations to determine if the current operation is proceeding according to the commander's intent and if future operations are supportable. (FM 3-0)

D-34. The OPSEC estimate contains up-to-date, OPSEC-related information; and the OPSEC officer updates it continuously throughout the operation. In a time-constrained environment, a current OPSEC estimate may be the only readily available source of OPSEC-related information. The OPSEC estimate contains—

- Probable threat picture of friendly forces.
- Threat collection capabilities.
- Current EEFI.
- OPSEC indicators.
- OPSEC measures in effect.
- Contemplated OPSEC measures.

This page intentionally left blank.

Glossary

The glossary lists acronyms with Army, multi-Service, or joint definitions and other selected terms. Terms for which FM 3-37 is the proponent manual (the authority) are marked with an asterisk (*).

SECTION I – ACRONYMS AND ABBREVIATIONS

AA&E	arms, ammunition, and explosives
AC2	airspace command and control
ACP	air control point
ACR	Armored Cavalry Regiment
ADAM	air defense airspace management
ADW	air defense warning
AMD	air and missile defense
AML	area medical laboratory
AO	area of operations
AR	Army regulation
ARNG	Army National Guard
ARNGUS	Army National Guard of the United States
AT	antiterrorism
attn	attention
BAE	brigade aviation element
BCCS	battlefield command and control system
BCT	brigade combat team
BHL	battle handover line
C	confidential
C2	command and control
CA	civil affairs
CAIP	critical asset identification process
CAL	critical asset list
CARVER	criticality, accessibility, recuperability, vulnerability, effect, and recognizability
CAT	category
CBRN	chemical, biological, radiological, and nuclear
CBRNE	chemical, biological, radiological, nuclear, and high-yield explosives
CBT	combat
CCIR	commander's critical information requirements
CIS	constant surveillance service (single noncleared driver)

CJCSI	Chairman of the Joint Chiefs of Staff Instruction
CMO	civil-military operations
CND	computer network defense
COA	course of action
CONUS	continental United States
CRM	composite risk management
CSC	convoy support center
CU	see you
DA	Department of the Army
DAL	defended asset list
DCIP	Defense Critical Infrastructure Program
DDP	dual driver protective service (dual interim cleared drivers)
DISN	Defense Information Systems Network
DIV	division
DOD	Department of Defense
DODD	Department of Defense directive
DODI	Department of Defense instruction
DOS	Department of State
DP	decision point
DSCA	defense support of civil authorities
EA	engagement area
E. coli	Escherichia coli
EEFI	essential elements of friendly information
ENY	enemy
EO	explosive ordnance
EOD	explosive ordnance disposal
EXC	exclusive use of the vehicles
FEBA	forward edge of the battle area
FEMA	Federal Emergency Management Agency
FHP	force health protection
FM	field manual
FMI	field manual interim
FOB	forward operating base
FPCON	force protection condition
G	guard
G-2	assistant chief of staff, intelligence
G-3	assistant chief of staff, operations
G-5	assistant chief of staff, civil affairs
G-6	assistant chief of staff, signal
G-7	assistant chief of staff, information engagement
G-9	assistant chief of staff, civil affairs operations

HRP	high-risk personnel
IDN	initial distribution number
IE	information engagement
IED	improvised explosive device
IFF	identification, friend or foe
inc	incorporated
INFOCON	information operations condition
IPB	intelligence preparation of the battlefield
ISG	isolated Soldier guidance
ISR	intelligence, surveillance, and reconnaissance
J3	Operations Directorate
JCOB	joint contingency operations base
JFIRE	A pocket-size, quick-reference guide for requesting fire support in accordance with approved joint tactics, techniques, and procedures
JP	joint publication
LRA	local reproduction authorized
ltd	limited
MANSCEN	Maneuver Support Center
MCG	mobile command group
MDMP	military decisionmaking process
MEB	maneuver enhancement brigade
METT-TC	mission, enemy, terrain and weather, troops and support available, time available, and civil considerations
MND-B	multinational division–Baghdad
MOE	measure of effectiveness
MOP	measure of performance
MOPP	mission-oriented protective posture
MP	military police
MSHARPP	mission, symbolism, history, accessibility, recognizability, population, and proximity
MSR	main supply route
NA	not applicable
NAI	named area of interest
NASAMS	Norweigian Advanced, Surface-to-Air Missile System
NDMS	National Disaster Medical System
NETOPS	network operations
NGO	nongovernmental organization
OAKOC	observation and fields of fire, avenues of approach, key terrain, obstacles, and cover and concealment
OCONUS	outside the continental United States
OE	operational environment
OPLAN	operation plan

OPORD	operation order
OPSEC	operations security
P	pilferable
PATRIOT	Phased Array Tracking Radar to Intercept of Target
PIR	priorirty intelligence requirements
PL	phase line
PMESII-PT	political, military, economic, social, information, infrastructure, physical environment, and time
PR	personnel recovery
PSS	protective security service (secret cleared drivers)
PVNTMED	preventive medicine
ROE	rules of engagement
RSO&I	reception, staging, onward movement, and integration
RSP	render-safe procedures
S	secret; screen
S-3	operations staff officer
S-4	logistics staff officer
S-6	signal staff officer
SATCOM	satellite communications
SEV	security escort vehicle service
SOP	standing operating procedure
SNS	satellite navigation system
SPT	support
STRATCOM	Strategic Command
SUST	sustainment
TAC	tactical
TCF	tactical combat force
TCP	traffic control post
TIM	toxic industrial material
TLP	troop-leading procedures
TOC	tactical operations center
TPS	transportation protective services
TRP	target reference point
TTP	tactics, techniques, and procedures
U	unclassified
UFC	unified facilities criteria
U.S.	United States
USAR	U.S. Army Reserve
USCENTCOM	U.S. Central Command
USNORTHCOM	U.S. Northern Command
UXO	unexploded ordnance

VA	vulnerability assessment
WFF	warfighting function
WMD	weapons of mass destruction

SECTION II – TERMS

*base camp

An evolving military facility that supports the military operations of a deployed unit and provides the necessary support and services for sustained operations.

*critical asset list

A prioritized list of assets that should be protected; it is normally identified by the phase of an operation and approved by the commander.

*critical asset security

The protection and security of personnel and physical assets and/or information analyzed and deemed essential to the operation and success of the mission and the required resources for protection.

*defended asset list

A listing of those assets from the critical asset list, prioritized by the commander, to be defended with the resources available.

*fratricide

The unintentional killing of friendly personnel by friendly firepower.

*operational area security

A form of active security operations conducted to protect friendly forces, installations, routes, and actions within an area of operations.

*operations security measures

Methods and means to gain and maintain essential secrecy about essential elements of friendly information.

*protection

(Army) The preservation of the effectiveness of mission-related military and nonmilitary personnel, equipment, facilities, information, and infrastructure deployed or located within or outside the boundaries of a given operational area.

protection

(Joint) 1. Preservation of the effectiveness and survivability of mission-related military and nonmilitary personnel, equipment, facilities, information, and infrastructure deployed or located within or outside the boundaries of a given operational area. 2. In space usage, active and passive defensive measures to ensure that United States and friendly space systems perform as designed by seeking to overcome an adversary's attempts to negate them and to minimize damage if negation is attempted. (JP 3-11)

This page intentionally left blank.

References

SOURCES USED
These are the sources quoted or paraphrased in this publication.

ARMY PUBLICATIONS

AR 40-35. *Dental Readiness and Community Oral Health Protection.* 2 August 2004.

AR 40-656. *Veterinary Surveillance Inspection of Subsistence.* 28 August 2006.

AR 385-10. *Army Safety Program.* 23 August 2007.

AR 600-8-101. *Personnel Processing (In-, Out-, Soldier Readiness, Mobilization, and Deployment Processing).* 18 July 2003.

DA Pamphlet 385-10. *Army Safety Program.* 23 May 2008.

FM 1-02. *Operational Terms and Graphics.* 21 September 2004.

FM 2-0. *Intelligence.* 17 May 2004.

FM 3-0. *Operations.* 27 February 2008.

FM 3-07. *Stability Operations.* 6 October 2008.

FM 3-09.32. *(JFIRE) Multi-Service Tactics, Techniques, and Procedures for the Joint Application of Firepower.* 20 December 2007.

FM 3-11. *Multiservice Tactics, Techniques, and Procedures for Nuclear, Biological, and Chemical Defense Operations.* 10 March 2003.

FM 3-11.3. *Multiservice Tactics, Techniques, and Procedures for Chemical, Biological, Radiological, and Nuclear Contamination Avoidance.* 2 February 2006.

FM 3-11.4. *Multiservice Tactics, Techniques, and Procedures for Nuclear, Biological, and Chemical (NBC) Protection.* 2 June 2003.

FM 3-11.5. *Multiservice Tactics, Techniques, and Procedures for Chemical, Biological, Radiological, and Nuclear Decontamination.* 4 April 2006.

FM 3-11.21. *Multiservice Tactics, Techniques, and Procedures for Chemical, Biological, Radiological, and Nuclear Consequence Management Operations.* 1 April 2008.

FM 3-11.34. *Multiservice Tactics, Techniques, and Procedures for Installation CBRN Defense.* 6 November 2007.

FM 3-13. *Information Operations: Doctrine, Tactics, Techniques, and Procedures.* 28 November 2003.

FM 3-19.1. *Military Police Operations.* 22 March 2001.

FM 3-19.30. *Physical Security.* 8 January 2001.

FM 3-20.15. *Tank Platoon.* 22 February 2007.

FM 3-34. *Engineer Operations.* 2 April 2009.

FM 3-34.2. *Combined-Arms Breaching Operations.* 31 August 2000.

FM 3-36. *Electronic Warfare in Operations.* 25 February 2009.

FM 3-50.1. *Army Personnel Recovery.* 10 August 2005.

FM 3-90. *Tactics.* 4 July 2001.

FM 3-90.31. *Maneuver Enhancement Brigade Operations.* 26 February 2009.

FM 3-100.21. *Contractors on the Battlefield.* 3 January 2003.

FM 4-01.45. *Multi-Service Tactics, Techniques, and Procedures for Tactical Convoy Operations.* 5 January 2009.

FM 4-02.7. *Multiservice Tactics, Techniques, and Procedures for Health Service Support in a Chemical, Biological, Radiological, and Nuclear Environment.* 15 July 2009.

FM 4-02.17. *Preventive Medicine Services.* 28 August 2000.

FM 4-02.18. *Veterinary Services Tactics, Techniques, and Procedures.* 30 December 2004.

FM 4-02.19. *Dental Service Support in a Theater of Operations.* 1 March 2001.

FM 4-02.51. *Combat and Operational Stress Control.* 6 July 2006.

FM 5-19. *Composite Risk Management.* 21 August 2006.

FM 5-103. *Survivability.* 10 June 1985.

FM 5-415. *Fire-Fighting Operations.* 9 February 1999.

FM 6-20-10. *Tactics, Techniques, and Procedures for the Targeting Process.* 8 May 1996.

FM 7-15. *The Army Universal Task List.* 27 February 2009.

FM 44-100. *U.S. Army Air and Missile Defense Operations.* 15 June 2000.

FMI 3-35. *Army Deployment and Redeployment.* 15 June 2007.

FMI 3-90.10. *Chemical, Biological, Radiological, Nuclear, and High Yield Explosives Operational Headquarters.* 24 January 2008.

JOINT AND DEPARTMENT OF DEFENSE PUBLICATIONS

CJCSI 3121.01B. Standing Rules of Engagement/Standing Rules for the Use of Force for U.S. Forces. 13 June 2005.

DOD 4500.9-R. *Defense Transportation Regulations Part II: Cargo Movement.* November 2004.

DODD 5525.5. *DoD Cooperation with Civilian Law Enforcement Officials.* 15 January 1986.

JP 1. *Doctrine for the Armed Forces of the United States.* 2 May 2007.

JP 1-02. *Department of Defense Dictionary of Military and Associated Terms.* 12 April 2001.

JP 3-0. *Joint Operations.* 17 September 2006.

JP 3-01. *Countering Air and Missile Threats.* 5 February 2007.

JP 3-09. *Joint Fire Support.* 13 November 2006.

JP 3-10. *Joint Security Operations in Theater.* 1 August 2006.

JP 3-11. *Operations in Chemical, Biological, Radiological, and Nuclear (CBRN) Environments.* 26 August 2008.

JP 3-13. *Information Operations.* 13 February 2006.

JP 3-13.1. *Electronic Warfare.* 25 January 2007.

JP 3-27. *Homeland Defense.* 12 July 2007.

JP 3-28. *Civil Support.* 14 September 2007.

JP 3-30. *Command and Control for Joint Air Operations.* 5 June 2003.

JP 3-33. *Joint Task Force Headquarters.* 16 February 2007.

JP 3-34. *Joint Engineer Operations.* 12 February 2007.

JP 3-35. *Deployment and Redeployment Operations.* 7 May 2007.

JP 3-40. *Combating Weapons of Mass Destruction.* 10 June 2009.

JP 3-50. *Personnel Recovery.* 5 January 2007.

JP 3-52. *Joint Doctrine for Airspace Control in the Combat Zone.* 30 August 2004.

JP 4-02. *Health Service Support.* 31 October 2006.

JP 6-0. *Joint Communications System.* 20 March 2006.

OTHER PUBLICATIONS

Title 5, United States Code, Section 552.

Title 5, United States Code, Section 552a.

Title 10, United States Code.

Title 10, United States Code. Section 331-335.

Title 28, United States Code, Section 1385.

Title 32, United States Code.

DOCUMENTS NEEDED

These documents must be available to the intended users of this publication. DA forms are available on the Army Publishing Directorate Web site (www.apd.army.mil). DD forms are available on the OSD web site (www.dtc.mil/whs/directives/infomgt/forms/formsprogram.htm).

DA Form 2028. *Recommended Changes to Publications and Blank Forms.*

DD Form 1833. *Isolated Personnel Report (LRA).*

RELATED PUBLICATIONS

These sources contain relevant supplemental information.

ARMY PUBLICATIONS

AR 75-15. *(O)Policy for Explosive Ordnance Disposal.* 22 February 2005.

AR 525-13. *(O)Antiterrorism.* 11 September 2008.

AR 530-1. *(O)Operations Security (OPSEC).* 19 April 2007.

FM 1. *The Army.* 14 June 2005.

FM 3-05.40. *Civil Affairs Operations.* 29 September 2006.

FM 3-34.170. *Engineer Reconnaissance.* 25 March 2008.

FM 3-52. *Army Airspace Command and Control in a Combat Zone.* 1 August 2002.

FM 3-100.4. *Environmental Considerations in Military Operations.* 15 June 2000.

FM 4-02. *Force Health Protection in a Global Environment.* 13 February 2003.

FM 4-30.51. *Unexploded Ordnance (UXO) Procedures.* 13 July 2006.

FM 5-0. *Army Planning and Orders Production.* 20 January 2005.

FM 6-0. *Mission Command: Command and Control of Army Forces.* 11 August 2003.

FMI 2-01.301. *Specific Tactics, techniques, and Procedures and Applications for Intelligence Preparation of the Battlefield.* 31 March 2009.

FMI 3-01.50. *Air Defense and Airspace Management Cell Operations.* 27 February 2007.

FMI 5-0.1. *The Operations Process.* 31 March 2006.

STRATCOM Directive 527-1. *Operations, Planning, and Command and Control: Department of Defense (DOD) Information Operations Condition (INFOCON) System Procedures.* 27 January 2006.

TC 1-400. *Brigade Aviation Element Handbook.* 27 April 2006.

JOINT AND DEPARTMENT OF DEFENSE PUBLICATIONS

DOD O-2000.12-H. *(O)DOD Antiterrorism Handbook.* 1 February 2004.

DOD 3020.45-V1. *Defense Critical Infrastructure Program (DCIP): DOD Mission-Based Critical Asset Identification Process (CAIP).* 24 October 2008.

DOD 3020.45-V2. *Defense Critical Infrastructure Program (DCIP): DCIP Remediation Planning.* 28 October 2008.

DODI 2000.16. *DoD Antiterrorism (AT) Standards.* 2 October 2006.

DODI 3020.45. *Defense Critical Infrastructure Program (DCIP) Management.* 21 April 2008.

GTA 90-01-010. *(O)Joint Contingency Operations Base (JCOB) Force Protection Handbook.* October 2007.

JP 3-07.2. *(O)Antiterrorism.* 14 April 2006.

JP 3-13.3. *Operations Security.* 29 June 2006.

UFC 4-010-01. *DoD Minimum Antiterrorism Standards for Buildings.* 8 October 2003.

UFC 4-010-02. *DoD Minimum Antiterrorism Standoff Distances for Buildings.* 8 October 2003.

UFC 4-022-01. *Security Engineering: Entry Control Facilities/Access Control Points.* 25 May 2005.

OTHER PUBLICATIONS

Darley, William M. "Clausewitz's Theory of War and Information Operations." *Joint Force Quarterly.* January 2006.

Hawley, John K., PhD. "PATRIOT Fratricides: The Human Dimension Lessons of Operation Iraqi Freedom." *Air Defense Artillery.* January–March 2006.

Riehn, Richard K. *1812: Napoleon's Russian Campaign.* New York: McGraw-Hill, 1990.

Von Clausewitz, Carl. *On War.* New York: Penguin Classics, 1982. Published in Pelican Classics, 1968. This translation published by Routledge & Kegan Paul Ltd 1908. Von Krieg, published 1832.

Wong, Leonard and Gerras, Stephen. *CU @ The FOB: How the Forward Operating Base is Changing the Life of Combat Soldiers.* <http://www.strategicstudiesinstitute.army.mil/>. March 2006.

Zucchino, David. *Thunder Run: The Armored Strike to Capture Baghdad.* New York: Atlantic Monthly Press, 2004.

READINGS RECOMMENDED

These readings contain relevant supplemental information.

Army Directive 2008-02. *Army Protection.* 9 April 2008.

Index

This page intentionally left blank.

By order of the Secretary of the Army:

GEORGE W. CASEY, JR.
General, United States Army
Chief of Staff

Official:

JOYCE E. MORROW
Administrative Assistant to the
Secretary of the Army
0925208

DISTRIBUTION:

Active Army, Army National Guard, and U.S. Army Reserve: To be distributed in accordance with the initial distribution number (IDN) 110512, requirements for FM 3-37.

www.ingramcontent.com/pod-product-compliance
Lightning Source LLC
Chambersburg PA
CBHW080206300326
41934CB00038B/3390